EXPLORING
Prosperity
Preaching

Biblical Health, Wealth, & Wisdom

Debra J. Mumford

Foreword by DeForest B. Soaries Jr.

JUDSON PRESS
PUBLISHERS SINCE 1824

Join our mailing list for updates and special offers.
www.judsonpress.com/mailing_list.cfm

Exploring Prosperity Preaching

Judson Press has made every effort to trace the ownership of all quotes. In the event of a question arising from the use of a quote, we regret any error made and will be pleased to make the necessary correction in future printings and editions of this book.

Interior design by Crystal Devine.
Cover design by Wendy Ronga, Hampton Design Group.

Library of Congress Cataloging-in-Publication data
  Mumford, Debra J.
    Exploring prosperity preaching : biblical health, wealth & wisdom / Debra J. Mumford ; foreword by DeForest B. Soaries, Jr. -- 1st ed.
      p. cm.
    Includes bibliographical references (p.   ).
    ISBN 978-0-8170-1708-8 (pbk. : alk. paper) 1. African Americans--Religion. 2. Faith movement (Hagin) 3. Wealth--Religious aspects--Christianity. 4. Preaching. I. Title.
  BR563.N4M86 2012
  241'.6808996073--dc23
                           2011051583

Printed in the U.S.A.

First Edition, 2012.

Contents

Foreword

Early in my current pastorate, a church member came to see me. After a few minutes looking around my office, she turned to me and exclaimed: "Now I know your problem. You have too many books!" This prayerful and faithful lady had concerns about my leadership. She felt that, despite my intelligence and giftedness, I lacked "the anointing." But she was relieved because she now knew what to pray—"Please, God! Deliver our pastor from the shackles of all of those books!" I didn't need all of that stuff I studied in seminary. The anointing would enable me to teach people how to prosper.

I was not in the least bit surprised by that encounter, and she was not alone in the congregation in mixing prosperity theology with our Baptist faith. Like many devout Christians todays, these church members saw no contradiction between our biblically based doctrine and their overtly "Word of Faith" and prosperity gospel leanings. And why would they? The popular preachers who dominate the television networks have long invited Christians to experience a gospel that allows them to "prosper, even as [their] soul prospers"!

These celebrity prosperity preachers had identified some glaring weaknesses in the traditional church: aging clergy, declining membership, and lifeless worship. They took advantage of declining biblical literacy, and they tapped into a desire that many African Americans possessed in the post–Civil Rights era—a desire to redefine the role of church and faith. By the 1980s and 1990s black Christians were seeking leaders who would restore a sense of moral clarity, spiritual authenticity, and divine possibility. There was no Martin King on the horizon. But there were well-dressed, articulate, photogenic preachers (who were not prophetic enough to protest anything).

These preachers didn't preach elaborate, oratorical sermons laced with poetry and philosophy week after week. They abandoned the traditional hymns that included negative references such as "a wretch like me" and substituted praise songs that focused on joy and victory. They became inspirational speakers rather than prophetic preachers, offering a formula for tapping into divine power and accruing financial wealth. But they never discussed self-denial, personal sacrifice, or social justice.

In the preceding 250 years, the overwhelming majority of African American religious voices had come from prophetic leaders who employed an intuitive hermeneutic that produced a tradition emphasizing justice and righteousness. These black prophets preached a gospel of liberation from the same Bible that their oppressors used to justify their oppression.

And in the late eighteenth century, as black Christians separated from their white Christian brothers and sisters in response to their innate desire for equality and justice, the historically black church become the first major division of Christianity formed, not out of doctrinal disputes or political schism, but in response to an internal issue of injustice—that of racist ideology and practice within the church. Thus from the late 1700s until the late 1970s, black religious leaders had to possess a commitment to the pursuit of racial justice in order to be credible. The prophetic response to the social injustices faced by the black community was a core theological imperative.

Of course, outside the dominant prophetic tradition that has undergirded black struggle and survival, we have also seen charismatic leaders whose ministries have been overwhelmingly otherworldly or flamboyantly materialistic. The difference between then and now is that historically such religious leaders have been perceived as aberrations whose minority movements have existed only on the fringe of the black church as a whole.

Today cable and satellite television provides a ubiquitous presence for the prosperity message, allowing those ministries to experience phenomenal growth and to appear theologically mainstream. What's more, American culture overall has seen a shift in values that place emphasis on the individual over the group, earth over heaven, and success over service. This cultural shift has created a context that is receptive to prosperity theology.

Thankfully, many have already rejected the prosperity gospel—some because they are offended by the celebrity status and institutional successes of its leading proponents and others because they hear its false ring without having analyzed its teachings. And now, at last, a faithful Christian with a critical and discerning eye has accepted the call to dissect this movement in a manner that will help the entire Christian church. In *Exploring Prosperity Preaching*, homiletics professor Debra Mumford provides a thorough and integrally biblical critique of the growing prosperity gospel movement.

My mentor, the late Dr. Samuel D. Proctor, always said that proper Bible study asks three questions of every Scripture text:

1. *Is the text descriptive or prescriptive?* Does the text describe the reality of a particular time and place (e.g., smash an enemy's child against the stones), or is the text prescribing something for all time (e.g., love your neighbor as yourself)?

2. *Is the text a portrait or a photograph?* Does it use metaphor or hyperbole to "paint a picture" as a portrait artist would (e.g., Jesus sweat blood), or does it describe events plainly as a photographer documents reality (e.g., Jesus wept)?

3. *Is the text normative or germinative?* Does it offer a timeless truth (e.g., in Christ there is no slave or free), or is it something that seed-like must germinate and grow into a greater reality (e.g., slaves, obey your masters)?

Dr. Mumford observes that the biblical literalism common in prosperity preaching neglects our responsibility to ask these questions and thus allows preachers to proclaim feel-good messages that have no foundation in trustworthy hermeneutics.

The beauty of *Exploring Prosperity Preaching* is that Mumford is neither condemnatory nor judgmental in her analysis. She researches the origins of the Word of Faith movement, documents its core beliefs, and offers a constructive critique that is worthy of objective consideration. She also recognizes the prosperity movement's contributions to Christianity and challenges mainline churches to learn from its strengths and insights.

This is the most important book written about prosperity theology in the last thirty years. Adherents of prosperity preaching need this resource to understand the origins and implications of the gospel they preach. Mainline and prophetic preachers need this book because much of the thought, language, and expectations of Christian disciples today are being shaped by the popular prosperity message. And so laypeople also need this book to assist them in evaluating and understanding the messages that they hear. I believe this book is the key to saving black churches. Every preacher needs a copy in his or her hands.

REV. DR. DEFOREST B. SOARIES JR.
Author, *dfree™ Breaking Free from Financial Slavery*
Senior Pastor, First Baptist Church of Lincoln Gardens, New Jersey

Preface

Cedric Mumford, my brother, was my inspiration for studying prosperity preaching. Cedric was a member of a Word of Faith congregation in Goldsboro, North Carolina, for several years. While Cedric was attending that church, the pastor's financial demands on the members continually increased until they became unbearable. Members were told they not only had to give tithes and freewill offerings but also other offerings as requested by the pastor. Officers of the church, like Cedric, were required to give even more. Moreover, officers were expected to look prosperous by wearing nice clothes and driving expensive cars. The pastor's authority was conflated with biblical authority to such an extent that members felt that by obeying the pastor, they were obeying God. While the pastor got richer, some members gave until their homes went into foreclosure. Others, like Cedric, left and went to another church.

Cedric was fortunate to be able to go to a church with a pastor he could trust—our father. But some people had a difficult time keeping their faith in God after leaving the church, because blame for not being prosperous was placed, by the pastors of prosperity-preaching churches, squarely on their shoulders. According to some pastors, if they had had enough faith, they would have been rich rather than in foreclosure.

Our father's church, of which Cedric is currently a member, has also adopted prosperity theology. While growing up, I saw my father reading the books of Kenneth E. Hagin and Fred Price in his study. In his more than forty years of preaching the gospel, Rev. Jimmy A. Mumford wed the prosperity theology with the theology of his Missionary Baptist tradition. In recent years, prosperity theology has become a more prominent part of his theology. The difference between the approach my father takes to prosperity theology and the approach of Cedric's former pastor is that my father does not make financial demands on his members. He teaches prosperity theology but allows members to determine for themselves the level at which they would like to give to the church. He teaches his members to tithe and proclaims the blessings God promises to give when they sow seed. However, he does not mandate them to give at any particular level. Though he does not make financial demands on his members, he does insist that his members develop an unwavering faith in God.

The major strength of my father's ministry is his faith in God's ability to do all things, which he conveys to his congregation in his preaching, teaching, and prayers. When he prays for the sick and ministers to those who have lost hope in their futures, he stands firmly on his faith in God. He truly believes there is nothing God cannot do. He teaches his members never to confess doubt and unbelief. He never confesses doubt publicly or privately. The same faith that he teaches his members is the faith he lives at home. The faith he conveys every week in his sermons is the faith both of my parents live out in their daily lives. Though my father and many members of his church are financially comfortable, no one has gotten rich. My parents have lived in the same small house in Kinston, North Carolina, for more than forty years.

While they are not financially wealthy, they are physically healthy and rich in faith.

Cedric's divergent experiences in prosperity-preaching churches demonstrate the perils and strengths of prosperity theology. All preachers of the prosperity gospel teach their hearers that God promises them wealth and good physical health. To obtain the promises of God, believers must sow seed or give money to people or churches to whom God directs them. However, some preachers blame their hearers if hearers do not become wealthy. In the meantime, the church or ministry continues to prosper along with the preacher. Other prosperity ministries are led by sincere pastors who teach the prosperity gospel because they truly believe in God's ability to do all things—including making the faithful wealthy. Some of these preachers never become wealthy.

In the pages that follow, I offer critiques of prosperity theology and discuss many of its controversial tenets.

Acknowledgments

This book is a culmination of research I started while enrolled in the PhD program in homiletics at the Graduate Theological Union in Berkeley, California. The three people who served on my dissertation committee were instrumental in helping me shape the direction of the dissertation and subsequently this book. Judy Yates Siker helped to refine my approach to biblical hermeneutics. Milmon Harrison's knowledge of and research on the Word of Faith movement made him an invaluable resource and conversation partner throughout the project. Mary Donovan Turner pushed me to create a project that not only met the GTU's academic standards, but that also honored the African American prophetic preaching tradition. I thank them for believing in the efficacy of the work and for offering support and critique where needed.

I thank attendees and colleagues of the African American Religion Groups, Western Region of the American Academy of Religion, in Claremont, California, 2006, and Southeastern Commission for the Study of Religion in Greensboro, North Carolina, March 2009, for their feedback. Their questions and comments helped to sharpen the focus of the work.

While enrolled in the doctoral program at the GTU, I received financial and collegial support from Dr. Sharon Watson Flucker and the wonderful people at the Fund for Theological Education. Without their support, this work would not have been possible. Through FTE I met African American scholars from many different religious traditions and theological disciplines who have served as wonderful conversation partners over the years.

I also thank my good friend Terry Dyonzak, who tolerated me typing out the dissertation on my laptop in her kitchen in the wee hours of the morning when we had sold our home in California but had not yet moved to Louisville, Kentucky. Everyone needs at least one Terry in her or his life. I thank the Louisville Presbyterian Theological Seminary for having faith that I would complete the dissertation before I began my position there and for supporting me financially as I completed the project. I am also appreciative of two of my colleagues at LPTS, Susan Garrett and Amy Plantinga Pauw, for reading sections of the book and offering helpful suggestions.

And I thank my parents, Hazel and Jimmy Mumford, for their ongoing support. Most of all, I thank Africa S. Hands for being a beloved partner and friend.

Introduction

Every day millions of people in the United States, Australia, Kenya, England, Brazil, Canada, Ukraine, and many other countries are able to turn on their televisions, download podcasts on iTunes, and visit popular websites to hear their favorite preachers share the "prosperity gospel." Prosperity gospel, also known as Word of Faith preaching, is a Christian theology whose signature teaching is that God wants believers to be rich and enjoy good physical health. To realize wealth and good health, believers need only believe in the promises of God and be obedient to God's word.

Word of Faith Controversy

To say that the preaching of the Word of Faith movement is controversial is a bit of an understatement. However, the reasons for controversy are varied. For some in charismatic or evangelical circles, the theology of the Word of Faith movement raises doctrinal concerns. Charismatic/evangelical detractors contend that Word of Faith preaching is heretical because it espouses New Thought metaphysical teachings

such as "positive confession," "visualization," "inner healing," and "positive thinking," which they believe to contra-
dict orthodox Christian doctrine.[1]

Others inside and outside of charismatic/evangelical circles
are primarily concerned about Word of Faith hermeneutics
or biblical interpretation. For these hermeneutical critics, the
practice of interpreting texts out of their historical and literary contexts enables Word of Faith preachers to justify their
consistent messages of prosperity.[2]

For others, social justice is the main concern. Some proponents of social justice are disturbed that preachers of the
Word of Faith movement get rich at the expense of their poor
congregants.[3] The poor not only listen to Word of Faith messages but also donate money to Word of Faith ministries with
the hope that when they give to God according to the instructions of the preacher, they will reap a hundredfold return on
their money. The tithes and offerings of members of prosperity churches, including the poor, pay for the mansions, Gulf-
stream jets, and Rolls-Royces of preachers of large ministries.
These poor masses, who have not been able to realize their
desires for financial prosperity while operating within their
local social economies, hope that by following the laws of the
divine economy explicated weekly by Word of Faith preachers, they will finally have all of their financial needs met. They
also hope to receive the desires of their hearts in the form of
material goods.

Social justice is also an issue because prosperity theology
ignores discrimination, racism, sexism, classism, and other
justice concerns in the larger society. In some cases, injustice
is not only overlooked in prosperity churches but is sometimes supported.

A concern for biblical interpretation and social justice are
at the heart of this project. Does God truly promise in biblical texts that all believers can be rich? Does God promise all
believers perfect physical health? Are Word of Faith preachers simply taking advantage of sincere people who want to

believe that they can achieve the American dream of wealth and prosperity through the promises of God? In this book I seek answers to these questions by examining the theology of prominent Word of Faith preachers to understand how they arrive at their message of prosperity. It is with biblical interpretation and social justice in mind that I have also chosen to compare and contrast Word of Faith preaching with black prophetic preaching.

My Preparation for Writing This Book

This book is intended to provide Word of Faith adherents with a critical analysis of the theology and alternative ways of understanding God in relation to financial prosperity, physical health, and Christian social responsibility.

To understand how Word of Faith preachers are taught to interpret biblical texts, I enrolled in and completed a Bible Interpretation correspondence course at the Rhema Bible Training Center (RBTC) in Broken Arrow, Oklahoma. The school was founded by Kenneth E. Hagin and has trained pastors and laity of Word of Faith churches all over the world for active ministry. In addition to providing an overview of the Bible and synopses of each of the books, the course also taught students how to adjudicate biblical prophecy, how to understand the role of the anointing, how they can know the will of God, how to turn hopeless situations around, and how to live a *zoe*, or God, kind of life.

In January 2007 I attended five worship services in the World Dome of Creflo Dollar's World Changers Church International and in a small chapel on the church's campus. I also interviewed David Bernknoff, Creflo Dollar's publicist. Though a complete narrative of my site visit is not included in this book, the worship experiences provided essential first-hand knowledge of the worship context and overall ministry that allowed me to validate some information found during my research.

Throughout this book, the terms "prosperity theology," "prosperity gospel," and "Word of Faith theology" are used interchangeably to refer to the theology of the Word of Faith movement. I have not capitalized the word *word* when it refers to God's word, the Bible, to distinguish it from Jesus (the Word of God).

An Overview of the Book

Although the prosperity gospel is relatively new on the religious landscape, its worldwide media presence has enabled the dissemination of its message to people of all ages, ethnicities, races, and religious and denominational affiliations. We will closely examine the prosperity gospel to deconstruct its teachings. But first we need to understand how prosperity preaching evolved and learn about the people responsible for its existence. Therefore, chapter 1 provides an overview of the history of prosperity preaching, including people and movements that influenced its origins, such as E.W. Kenyon, Kenneth E. Hagin, and Oral Roberts. I survey African American preachers of New Thought, including Father Divine, Reverend Ike, and Johnnie Rae Colemon, and introduce contemporary Word of Faith ministers as well.

The next ten chapters outline the core teachings of the prosperity gospel. Each chapter bears a title that represents a frequently used phrase by prosperity preachers. The theology that undergirds each phrase is explained, and affirmations and critiques are included in a section titled "Sifting the Wheat from the Chaff" in each chapter. Biblical texts that prosperity preachers use to justify their teachings are included where applicable.

Chapter 2, "The Word of God Means Exactly What It Says," explores the biblical assumptions on which the prosperity gospel is based. Word of Faith preachers interpret the Bible using proof texting, typology, and propositional revelation.

I examine the rationale of literal interpretation and rejection of biblical exegesis. In the Sifting the Wheat from the Chaff section, I describe the dangers of interpretation without context. (I present an alternative interpretive approach in another chapter.)

Chapter 3 looks at the prosperity gospel's teaching that declares, "The world's economy is not your economy." According to Word of Faith theology, two economies exist in the world—the secular economy and God's divine economy. In the divine economy, believers become wealthy only by giving away what they have. Adherents are advised to ignore the realities of the world's economy and to believe that God will supply not only their needs but also the desires of their hearts. In Sifting the Wheat from the Chaff, I examine the potential consequences of ignoring secular realities, using prosperity preaching's role (as reported in some news articles) in the 2008 housing crisis as an example.

Chapter 4, "Poverty Is a Curse, and Jesus Was Not Poor," explores the Word of Faith contention that poverty is a curse. Since the central figure of the gospel (Jesus) cannot be under a curse, they also argue that Jesus was not poor. I will study the Scriptures used to support Word of Faith teachings about poverty, including how prosperity preachers offer alternate interpretations of biblical texts that describe Jesus' socioeconomic status. In Sifting the Wheat from the Chaff, I differentiate between the poor people as "cursed of God" and "poverty" as "a curse." I also offer an African American prophetic preaching perspective on Jesus' social status.

In chapter 5, I consider the "God is your source" teaching. While all preachers of Word of Faith theology contend that God is the source of all blessings, including finances, some preachers are more specific about the sources of wealth available for Christians. For example, some teach that "the wealth of sinners is laid up for the righteous." In order for the righteous to receive stored money, they literally need to cry out for it. In Sifting the Wheat from the Chaff, I offer an African American prophetic preaching perspective. I also offer a basic approach to biblical exegesis.

Chapter 6, "The Anointing Produces Victory," examines how the teachings of Kenneth E. Hagin, who believed in the power of the Holy Spirit (the anointing) to empower believers for ministry, have been adopted by Word of Faith preachers to teach that the anointing also empowers believers to prosper financially. I investigate interpretations of Joel 2:18–4:17, including the teachings of the Latter Rain movement. In Sifting the Wheat from the Chaff, I examine the concept of anointing in the Old Testament and present an African American prophetic preaching alternative.

In chapter 7, we will explore the Word of Faith teaching in the refrain "There is authority in the name of Jesus." Word of Faith preachers proclaim that believers should use that authority to create their own life realities. Essentially, adherents are taught that their lives are direct reflections of their verbal confessions. In Sifting the Wheat from the Chaff, I look into the dangers of misusing the concept of "authority" and offer an African American prophetic preaching perspective.

In chapter 8, "Claim Your Healing," I probe the Word of Faith assertion that believers need never be sick. Good physical health is a right of all Christians, and so believers have only to claim their good health in order to receive it. I highlight the Word of Faith interpretation of Isaiah 53:4-5 as it relates to God's promise of healing. In Sifting the Wheat from the Chaff, I offer an alternative interpretation of the Isaiah text and examine other healing texts. Using the testimony of Betty Price, wife of prosperity preacher Fred Price, I encourage readers to broaden their thinking about healing beyond the miraculous.

In chapter 9, "You Are the Righteousness of God," we will test the Word of Faith teaching that asserts that believers have been declared righteous in God's sight and therefore have at work in them the same unlimited ability and wisdom of God as Christ had. I contrast Word of Faith theology of the righteousness of God and the favor of God of prosperity preachers with that of Swiss reformer John Calvin. In Sifting the Wheat from the Chaff, I dissuade readers from conceiving of God as their personal valet.

In chapter 10, "Race Doesn't Matter," I examine the teachings of Word of Faith teacher Creflo Dollar Jr. on race. Building on the promise of the elusive American Dream, his teaching asserts that people no longer need to identify with their natural heritage (race) once they are born again, because they have a new spiritual heritage with which to identify. Identifying with a particular ethnic or racial group creates division in the church. I will contrast Word of Faith's theology of race with the teachings of evangelical and prophetic traditions. In Sifting the Wheat from the Chaff, I argue that racism is not a personal problem but a systemic issue.

Chapter 11 examines Word of Faith's belief that "living by the word of God eliminates social ills." Adherents say that all of society's issues of social injustice would be resolved if all people would convert to Christianity. Word of Faith's focus on individual conversion is indicative of the individualistic nature of prosperity theology. Believers are taught to make confessions (verbal claims to the promises of God) to God on behalf of themselves and their families rather than on behalf of others. I highlight the entitlement issues that result and compare and contrast these claims with those of black prophetic preaching.

In chapter 12, "Affirmations, Denouncements, and Reconstruction of Faith," I delineate the gifts that prosperity theology brings to Christendom, along with its shortcomings. I offer observations and insights about the primary beneficiaries of prosperity theology, draw conclusions about the value of and need for critical biblical interpretation and holistic theological education, and suggest approaches to reconstructing faith after rejecting the prosperity gospel. Finally, I appeal to all people of God to work for the resurgence of the African American prophetic preaching tradition.

Before closely examining the particulars of the theology of the Word of Faith movement, however, we will seek to understand its origins and the people who knowingly and unknowingly helped to develop it. That is our starting place in chapter 1.

NOTES

1. Dave Hunt, *Occult Invasion* (Eugene, OR: Harvest House, 1998), 17. See also John MacArthur, *Charismatic Chaos* (Grand Rapids: Zondervan, 1992), 322–53.

2. Andrew Perriman and World Evangelical Alliance Commission on Unity and Truth among Evangelicals, *Faith, Health and Prosperity: A Report on Word of Faith and Positive Confession Theologies by ACUTE* (Carlisle: Paternoster, 2003), 88–92.

3. Shayne Lee, *T. D. Jakes: America's New Preacher* (New York: New York University Press, 2005), 109.

CHAPTER 1

Prosperity Gospel in Context

The prosperity gospel has only existed in its current form since the 1960s; its roots, however, are deep and wide. It originated in the United States, which is known worldwide for the "American Dream," the belief that since the United States is the land of opportunity, anyone, regardless of race, creed, or color, can become wealthy by working hard and following the rules of the capitalistic system. People therefore come from all over the world in hopes of achieving financial prosperity for themselves and their families.

However, for many people who were born and raised in this country and whose ancestors have been United States citizens for centuries, the American Dream has remained elusive. Many have found, for myriad reasons, including obstacles systemic to capitalism itself, that they have not been able to realize the American dream of material wealth. The prosperity gospel teaches believers that where systems fail, God succeeds. Prosperity preachers tell their hearers that race, age, education, and class do not matter, that God does not care who you are or where you are from. If believers are faithful to the word of God and live their lives according to the word (as interpreted by prosperity preachers), they can be rich and have good health. It is this unqualified hope and optimism that make prosperity gospel so appealing. Believers are told that the God of the Bible—the same one who brought the Israelites out of Egypt and worked miracles in the lives of Abraham, Deborah, and Daniel—can work miracles in their lives as well.

As we trace the evolution of the prosperity gospel, we must first take a look at a movement that is responsible for shaping the thought processes of prosperity gospel adherents all over the world—New Thought.

New Thought Movement

In the eighteenth and nineteenth centuries, a very quiet movement began in New England under the leadership of a white clock maker named Phineas Parkhurst Quimby—a movement that would prove foundational for Word of Faith preaching.[1] This movement would become known as New Thought metaphysics or, more simply, New Thought.[2] The term *metaphysics* indicates a belief that individuals can control the circumstances of their lives by controlling their thinking.

Quimby, born in 1802, was particularly interested in mental healing. After being healed of tuberculosis, he was inspired to better understand the relationship between a person's physical illness and his or her thoughts.[3] He began to study and practice mesmerism (hypnosis) and eventually developed his own healing theories.[4] For example, in a short essay titled "Is Disease a Belief?" Quimby wrote of the relationship between the mind and disease:

> If I am sick, I am sick for my feelings are my sickness, and my sickness is my belief, and my belief is my mind; therefore all disease is in the mind or belief. Now as our belief or disease is made up of ideas which are matter, it is necessary to know what ideas we are in; for to cure the disease is to correct the error; and as

disease is what follows the error, destroy the cause, and the effect will cease.[5]

Quimby felt that by discovering the connection between the mind and disease, he had rediscovered the healing technique of Jesus.[6]

Out of the New Thought movement grew several other movements. Quimby's best-known student was Mary Baker Eddy, who founded Christian Science.[7] In turn, some of Eddy's students included Charles and Myrtle Fillmore, who founded the Unity School of Christianity; Malinda E. Cramer, who cofounded Divine Science; and Ernest Holmes, who founded Religious Science.[8] Over the years, proponents of New Thought taught that changing one's thinking could not only affect one's health but every aspect of one's life, including financial well-being.

More than a hundred years after Quimby developed New Thought, those teachings somehow found their way into the preaching of a Pentecostal minister from Texas named Kenneth Hagin.

New Thought and the Word of Faith Movement

Kenneth Erwin Hagin was born on August 20, 1917, in McKinney, Texas. He was a sickly child, bedridden with a deformed heart during most of his childhood. He was not expected to live very long. However, after reading Mark 5:34, which records Jesus' healing of the woman with the issue of blood, he was completely healed.[9] Soon after his healing, at the age of seventeen, Hagin began to preach.

After preaching for more than twenty years, Hagin converted to Pentecostalism from the Southern Baptist denomination because he wanted to fellowship with people who believed in divine healing.[10] In 1962 Hagin began preaching and teaching that reality was "created in the minds and affirmed in the speech of believers."[11] Though Hagin claimed that his teachings were inspired by the Holy Spirit, it is believed that Hagin actually plagiarized his teachings from E. W. Kenyon, an independent evangelist and Bible teacher.[12] In turn, Kenyon is believed to have adopted many of his teachings from Christian Science and New Thought.[13]

From the beginning of his ministry, Hagin used the media very effectively to spread his message. He moved to Tulsa, Oklahoma, and began broadcasting his teachings on his radio program, "Faith Seminar of the Air."[14] Hagin founded the Kenneth E. Hagin Evangelistic Association and published his teachings in a magazine called *Word of Faith*. Hence the Word of Faith movement was born.[15] In addition to his beliefs about healing and New Thought, Hagin integrated Pentecostalism into the movement by teaching his followers about the power of the Holy Spirit manifested through the gift of tongues and the anointing (empowerment of believers for ministry). Hagin also published over 120 books and numerous audiocassettes.

In addition to broadcasting his sermons on the radio and selling books and audiotapes espousing his theology, Hagin wanted to train and teach as many ministers as possible. Thus, he founded Rhema Correspondence School in 1968 and the Rhema Bible Training Center in 1974 (*rhema* meaning "word"). Through these educational endeavors, Hagin trained thousands of new Word of Faith preachers.

Hagin founded the Rhema Ministerial Association International (RMAI) in 1985.[16] The members of this association are usually graduates of Rhema Bible Training Center and are licensed or ordained by RMAI. In December 2010, 975 churches were listed as members.[17] Hagin's effective use of media and his teaching ministry at Rhema ensured the proliferation of his message to diverse audiences. Hagin died in 2003. His son, Kenneth W. Hagin, is currently president of Kenneth Hagin Ministries and pastor of Rhema Bible Church. Under his leadership, the work of training ministers and leaders in the Word of Faith theological tradition continues.

Real Father of the Word of Faith Movement

Many Word of Faith preachers readily acknowledge Kenneth E. Hagin to have been their mentor and the father of the Word of Faith movement. However, in his book, *A Different Gospel*, Dan McConnell argues that Essek William Kenyon is actually the father of the Word of Faith movement, since Hagin plagiarized Word of Faith doctrine directly from Kenyon. McConnell displays the writings of Kenyon and Hagin side by side to illustrate the degree of Hagin's plagiarism. McConnell contends that Kenyon is the founding father of the Faith movement because he originally wrote the teachings on which the Word of Faith movement is based.[18]

Essek William Kenyon was an evangelist, pastor, and teacher who was born in a lumber camp in Hadley Hills, New York, on April 24, 1867.[19] Because of his family's poverty, at the age of twelve, Essek began to work at a carpet mill twelve hours a day. During his teen years, Kenyon dreamed of becoming an actor. However, upon converting to Christianity at the age of seventeen while attending services at a Methodist church, Kenyon discerned that he was called to preach. He was given an exhorter's license by the Methodist Episcopal Church in Amsterdam, New York.[20] At the age of nineteen, he preached his first sermon.[21] His intellectual curiosity led him to explore philosophy and metaphysics. He attended services of a Unitarian minister and also received training at Emerson College of Oratory in Boston.

Kenyon spent much of his life pastoring churches throughout the United States. In 1898 he founded Bethel Bible Institute, where he trained students in evangelism, mission, and divine healing.[22] Choosing to operate on faith at the institute, Kenyon insisted that no teacher or department head ever receive a salary and no student ever be charged tuition.[23] Kenyon remained at Bethel for twenty-three years.[24] While there, Kenyon also published the monthly periodical *Reality*.[25] He resigned his superintendent position at Bethel in 1924 because of fiscal policy differences with the board.[26] After leaving Bethel, Kenyon pastored several small churches throughout the United States, including a church in California.

In 1931, at the age of sixty-four, Kenyon launched *Kenyon's Church of the Air*, a radio ministry.[27] He founded the Seattle Bible Institute in 1935. Shortly after opening the Institute, Kenyon also began to publish the paper *Kenyon's Herald of Life*. The circulation for this paper reached twenty thousand by the time of his death in Los Angeles in 1948.[28]

KENYON'S WRITINGS

Kenyon wrote and published sixteen books and two Bible courses. Many of Kenyon's books are compilations of articles written for *Kenyon's Herald of Life*[29] or edited transcripts of radio broadcasts.[30] They are based on his own Christian experiences and reflect his zeal for teaching and preaching. Currently his books are published by Kenyon's Gospel Publishing Society, which was managed by his daughter, Ruth Kenyon, until her death in 1993.

After Kenyon converted to Christianity, he experienced a period when he felt spiritually lost. Upon reflection, he determined that he was spiritually lost at that time because he had not received the teaching needed to ground him in the word as a new Christian. Not wanting other people to have similar experiences, Kenyon taught practical applications of the Bible to everyday life.[31] He established Bible schools, developed radio broadcasts, and published his teachings in periodicals and books. Kenyon considered the churches he pastored as "training centers to equip the saints."[32]

Kenyon taught courses that covered topics such as Bible exposition, public speaking, the art of personal contact (how to work with people), meeting facilitation, message preparation, testimony and prayer meeting leadership, and soul winning and evangelism.[33]

Seed-Faith Theology and the Divine Economy

While Kenyon's writings provided a theological foundation for the Word of Faith movement, Oral Roberts's seed-faith theology also became a very important component of the foundation.

One of the most important teachings of the Word of Faith movement is the *divine economy*, which was created and popularized by the late Oral Roberts. Roberts was an evangelist and healer and the founding president of Oral Roberts University in Tulsa, Oklahoma. He taught that the divine economy is an economic system based on the belief that God wants to provide God's people with material prosperity.[34] An alternative to the secular economy, the divine economy is activated by faith in the goodness of God and the law of sowing and reaping, or seed-faith.

Roberts's original doctrine of seed-faith is composed of three core principles, which if applied properly in the life of the believer are supposed to ensure that she or he will enjoy abundant life.[35] The first core principle is that Christians should turn their lives completely over to God by recognizing that God, not humanity, is the source of all their needs.[36] People who help Christians at various points in their lives are instruments of God. However, they are not the source of any blessings. God is the source.[37]

The second core principle is the principle of sowing and reaping.[38] Whatever the believer gives freely to God becomes a seed for God to multiply back to the believer in the form of their needs. When believers sow seeds of any kind—by giving of their talent, time, love, compassion, or money—they will receive those things in return. If believers want God to supply their financial needs, they need to give seed money to God for God to reproduce and multiply.[39] Roberts was very careful to differentiate seed-faith giving from tithing. Seed-faith giving is done *before* the miracle is manifested or the need has been met.[40] Tithing is done *after* one has been blessed by God financially.

Roberts also explained that giving to God means giving to the church or to someone to whom God directs the believer.[41] For example, there was a time when Roberts and his wife, Evelyn, were struggling to pay their rent. Roberts was led to give a seed-faith offering to God. After he gave the offering, a man who was a member of the church Roberts was pastoring gave Roberts an amount seven times the offering Roberts had given to the church. As a result, Roberts and his wife were able to stay in the house.[42]

The third core principle of seed-faith is to expect a miracle immediately after the seed is planted.[43] In order to expect a miracle, believers must release their faith in God by truly believing that God is going to grant them a miracle.[44]

Roberts advised believers to plant seeds that represent the miracles they need. For example, they should plant a seed of time if they need time or a seed of love if they need love. They can plant a seed of time by volunteering to help an individual or cause. They can sow a seed of love by showing the love of God to others in an act of kindness. Money seeds, however, can be planted to meet many types of needs. For example, Roberts recounted a testimony of a young woman who planted a financial seed for reconciliation in her marriage. The financial seed was the point of contact she needed to release her own faith. She and her husband did reconcile.

In addition to his seed-faith theology, Roberts was renowned for his ministry of divine healing. Roberts died in 2009.

Emergence of New Thought in Black Preaching

While Hagin and Roberts were continuing to develop their ministries, New Thought metaphysics was finding its way into African American religious communities. During the Great Migration (1915–1920), an estimated 1.5 million Southern blacks moved to Northern states to escape sharecropping, tenant farming, and abject poverty.[45] During this period,

Chicago's black population grew by 148 percent, Cleveland's by 307 percent, and Detroit's by 611 percent. Many blacks hoped to find employment in the North and new lives for themselves and their families.[46] One preacher who arose during this period was George Baker, better known as Father Major Jealous Divine or "Father Divine."[47] Father Divine established the Peace Mission movement in Sayville, Long Island, New York, in which he preached self-help and positive thinking; held his followers to a strict code of ethics, including no drinking, smoking, or drugs; prohibited racial prejudice and discrimination among those in the movement; and established small black businesses while urging his followers to patronize those businesses.[48] While Father Divine required his followers to maintain a strict standard of personal piety, he also encouraged a commitment to social justice. Divine's followers were urged to develop a plan for a "righteous government" in which equality for all would be realized and Jim Crow practices and lynching would be repealed.[49] Father Divine was known for his flamboyant appearance.

Another flamboyant preacher during this period was Charles Manuel Grace, also known as "Daddy Grace" or "Sweet Daddy Grace." Sweet Daddy Grace founded the House of Prayer for All People in 1919 in West Wareham, Massachusetts, in which he promised his people they could live the good life by "placing their trust, their faith, and most of their money in his hands."[50] Though the doctrine of the House of Prayer for All People is said to have resembled Pentecostalism, Daddy Grace also preached positive thinking.[51]

Johnnie Colemon and Frederick J. Eikerenkoetter II (Reverend Ike) were also preaching messages of self-reliance and individualism, while preachers of the civil rights movement preached messages about the need for solidarity and the power of unity in the face of injustice. However, the preaching of Ike and Colemon was more comprehensive than it appeared on the surface.

Rev. Dr. Johnnie Colemon is an ordained minister in the Unity tradition. After enrolling in the Unity School of

Christianity and being healed of an incurable disease, Colemon began to teach Unity principles of healing and positive thinking. In 1956 she founded the Christ Universal Temple in Chicago, which is currently the largest New Thought church in the world, with twenty thousand members.[52] Then and now, members are taught that a happy, healthy, and prosperous life is within reach of each individual who realizes that the kingdom of God is within her or him,[53] for "God . . . created God's people to be perfect, whole and complete, and fined and surrounded in and with prosperity."[54]

The late Rev. Dr. Frederick J. Eikerenkoetter II, better known as Reverend Ike, believed that all the problems of society began with the individual.[55] He preached a gospel of self-identity to get each person to believe in the "divinity or dignity within himself."[56] Reverend Ike founded the Miracle Temple in Boston in 1965 and the United Church and Science of Living Institute in 1969 to teach people how to live better lives through positive thinking. Though not formally a member of the New Thought movement, his teachings were an intersection between New Thought teachings and African American religious expressions.

While Father Divine, Sweet Daddy Grace, Rev. Johnnie Coleman, and Reverend Ike were the first black preachers to formally incorporate New Thought metaphysics into their preaching, many of today's black Word of Faith preachers acknowledge the teachings and preaching of Kenneth E. Hagin as a major influence on their own preaching ministries. One of the first and most prominent African American preachers to be influenced by Kenneth Hagin is Frederick K. C. Price.

FREDERICK K. C. PRICE

Though the Word of Faith movement is a predominantly Euro-American movement, African American preachers have also founded and currently serve as senior pastors of large Word of Faith congregations. One of the black pioneers and most widely renowned preachers of the Word of

Faith movement is Frederick K. C. Price. Price founded the Crenshaw Christian Center (CCC) in South Central Los Angeles in 1973.

As of September 2011, CCC's membership was more than twenty-two thousand.[57] In addition, in 1990 Dr. Price founded the Fellowship of Inner City Word of Faith Ministries (FICWFM), a ministerial association of independent churches from all over the United States and various countries. The purpose of the FICWFM is to "provide fellowship, leadership, guidance and a spiritual covering for those desiring a standard of excellence in ministry."[58]

In 2001 Price established a New York church, Crenshaw Christian Center East, which had a membership of fourteen hundred by September 2011.[59] CCC has educational facilities for preschool through grade twelve as well as a correspondence school.[60] Price's *Ever Increasing Faith* television and internet broadcasts reach more than 15 million households each week and air in fifteen of the twenty largest markets throughout the United States, according to recent Nielson ratings.[61]

Price readily admits that his faith was influenced by the teachings of Kenneth Hagin during a critical period of his ministry. "It was during this time that Betty [Price's wife] and I began to take the first steps to walk by faith, which has brought us to where we are today."[62] Price holds an honorary diploma from the Rhema Bible Training Center, and he named one of the buildings on the Crenshaw campus after Hagin.[63]

Price is a role model for all Word of Faith preachers in general and for black Faith preachers in particular. Though he has certainly thrived in the movement, he is not without controversy. The relationship between Hagin and Price changed in 1998 when Price began a preaching series and wrote books that attacked racism in the Christian church.[64] Price objected to Kenneth W. Hagin's teachings against interracial marriage. The senior Hagin defended his son's stance. Price severed all ties to his former mentor. He even removed Hagin's name from the building on the Crenshaw campus.[65]

Though Price was one of the first African American preachers of the Word of Faith movement, today he is one among hundreds, including Creflo Dollar Jr., pastor of World Changers International Ministries of College Park, Georgia, with a membership of twenty thousand; Bill Winston, founder and pastor of the Living Word Christian Center in Oak Park, Illinois, with a membership of more than nineteen thousand; and Leroy Thompson Sr., pastor of Word of Life Christian Center in Darrow, Louisiana, with a membership of seventeen hundred.

Despite being in existence only since the 1960s, largely because of its vast media presence, prosperity theology has been adopted by thousands of pastors and laypeople both inside and outside the movement. Since prosperity theology is so pervasive, we will examine its teachings closely for understanding, beginning with its view of Scripture.

NOTES

1. Darnise C. Martin, *Beyond Christianity: African Americans in a New Thought Church* (New York: New York University Press, 2005), 12.

2. It is important to note this movement because of the influence New Thought teachings have on the preaching of the Word of Faith movement.

3. Martin, *Beyond Christianity*, 12.

4. Ibid.

5. Phineas Parkhurst Quimby, *Is Disease a Belief?* Phineas Parkhurst Quimby Resource Center. http://www.ppquimby.com/articles/is_disease_a_belief.htm (accessed January 4, 2012).

6. Martin, *Beyond Christianity*, 13.

7. Ibid., 14.

8. Ibid., 15–16.

9. Kenneth E. Hagin, *New Thresholds of Faith* (Tulsa: Rhema Bible Church, 1985), 3–4.

10. Kenneth E. Hagin, "Healing and Miracles through United Prayer," *Word of Faith*, August 1998, 4–8.

11. Milmon F. Harrison, *Righteous Riches: The Word of Faith Movement in Contemporary African American Religion* (New York: Oxford University Press, 2005), 6.

12. Ibid., 5–6.

13. D. R. McConnell, *A Different Gospel: A Historical and Biblical Analysis of the Modern Faith Movement* (Peabody, MA: Hendrickson, 1988), 30.

14. Harrison, *Righteous Riches*, 6.

15. Ibid.

16. Ibid.

17. Kenneth Hagin Ministries, "Rhema Ministerial Association International Church Guide," *Word of Faith*, August 2010, 15–22.

18. McConnell, *A Different Gospel*, 57.

19. Joe McIntyre, *E. W. Kenyon and His Message of Faith: The True Story* (Orlando: Creation House, 1997), 1.

20. Ibid., 3.

21. Richard Riss, "Essek William Kenyon," in *Dictionary of Pentecostal and Charismatic Movements*, ed. Stanley M. Burgess and Gary B. McGee (Grand Rapids: Zondervan, 1988), 517.

22. Ibid., 25. Kenyon added the ministry of healing to his cadre of ministries after he was healed of peritonitis, an inflammation of the membrane lining the abdominal cavity. Thereafter, healing became a major part of his ministry.

23. McConnell, *A Different Gospel*, 32.

24. After moving several times geographically and merging with several theological institutions such as Providence Bible Institute in Providence, Rhode Island, and Gordon College in Wenham, Massachusetts, the once Bethel Bible Institute is now subsumed into the Gordon-Conwell Theological Seminary of South Hamilton, Massachusetts. See McIntyre, *E. W. Kenyon*, 128.

25. Ibid., 106.

26. Ibid., 126.

27. Dale H. Simmons, *E. W. Kenyon and the Postbellum Pursuit of Peace, Power and Plenty*, Studies in Evangelicalism, no. 13 (Lanham, MD: Scarecrow, 1997), 44. Kenyon moved to Seattle after his second wife, Alice, filed for divorce. Alice Kenyon charged that Kenyon tried to have sex with his secretary and other women. When Kenyon left Los Angeles, his reputation was severely sullied. At this point is his career, rather than traveling extensively to spread the gospel as he had in earlier years, he concentrated on publishing his books and expanding his radio ministry.

28. McIntyre, *E. W. Kenyon*, 173.

29. Ibid.

30. McConnell, *A Different Gospel*, 33.

31. McIntyre, *E. W. Kenyon*, 108.

32. Ibid., 109.

33. Ibid., 149.

34. Andrew Perriman and World Evangelical Alliance, Commission on Unity and Truth among Evangelicals, *Faith, Health and Prosperity: A Report on Word of Faith and Positive Confession Theologies by ACUTE* (Carlisle: Paternoster, 2003), 51.

35. Oral Roberts, *The Miracle of Seed-Faith* (Tulsa: Oral Roberts Ministries, 1970), 37.

36. Ibid., 15.

37. Ibid.

38. Ibid., 23.

39. Ibid., 21. Roberts cited Luke 6:38 as evidence of the need to give: "Give, and it shall be given unto you; good measure, pressed down, and shaken together, and running over, shall men give into your bosom. For with the same measure that ye mete withal it shall be measured to you again" (KJV).

40. Ibid., 27–28.

41. Ibid., 57.

42. Ibid., 18. Roberts also saw no conflict of interest in accepting a personal offering from a church member.

43. Ibid., 29–30.

44. Ibid., 30–31.

45. S. Mintz, "The Great Migration," 2003, http://www.digitalhistory.uh.edu/database/article_display.cfm?HHID=443 (accessed July 4, 2006).

46. Ibid.

47. Harrison, *Righteous Riches*, 133.

48. George Eaton Simpson, *Black Religions in the New World* (New York: Columbia University Press, 1978), 266.

49. Ibid., 268.

50. Harrison, *Righteous Riches*, 133.

51. Simpson, *Black Religions*, 266.

52. Johnnie Colemon, "What We Believe" Christ Universal Temple, 1997, www.cutemplelife.org. Navigate to "About Us" and then "What We Believe" for more information. (accessed January 4, 2012).

53. Ibid.

54. Joy Bennett Kinnon, "Pastor: Johnnie Colemon—The Many-Splendored Faces of Today's Black Woman," Johnson Publishing, March 1997, http://www.findarticles.com/p/articles/mi_m1077/is_n5_v52/ai_19201542 (accessed December 13, 2011).

55. Charles V. Hamilton, *The Black Preacher in America* (New York: Morrow, 1972), 204.

56. Ibid.

57. Apostle Price Bio, Ever Increasing Faith Ministries, Los Angeles, http://www.crenshawchristiancenter.net/drprice.aspx?id=876 (accessed September 18, 2011).

58. Ibid.

59. History of CCC East, Ever Increasing Faith Ministries, Los Angeles, http://www.crenshawchristiancentereast.org/index.php?option=com_content&view=article&id=44&Itemid=60 (accessed September 18, 2011).

60. Apostle Price Bio.

61. Ibid.

62. Ibid.

63. Harrison, *Righteous Riches*, 163.

64. Ibid.

65. Ibid.

CHAPTER 2

The Word of God Means Exactly What It Says

At a Southwest Believer's Convention in Fort Worth, Texas, minister and evangelist Jesse Duplantis[1] told his hearers, "Any Scripture you read, you ought to be inspired, because it is coming from the lips of God." To make his case, Duplantis cited 2 Timothy 3:16, "All scripture is inspired by God and is useful for teaching, for reproof, for correction, and for training in righteousness."

Duplantis and other Word of Faith preachers teach their followers that the Bible is the literal word of God, representing an exact and flawless record of what God spoke directly to the people who recorded it. Duplantis inherited his view of the Bible from a long line of preachers who go all the way back to E. W. Kenyon. Therefore, we can better understand Duplantis's declaration when we examine Kenyon's understanding of Scripture, his rejection of biblical exegesis, and his approaches to interpretation. Since many believe Kenneth Hagin is the father of the Word of Faith movement, we will also examine how Hagin interpreted texts and how preachers are trained at Rhema Bible Training Center.

E. W. Kenyon and Biblical Exegesis

Kenyon believed that people could know God only by reading the Bible. It is through the believer's knowledge of God's
word and the promises therein that they can begin to understand who God is and what God has done for them through
Jesus Christ. Kenyon taught that the Bible is a "perfect book"
and it is only in the "perfect" word that God can be revealed
to humanity.[2]

During Kenyon's lifetime, various forms of biblical exegesis that were dominating European theology made their
way into theological seminaries and divinity schools in the
United States. Biblical exegesis is a critical explanation of a
biblical text or a biblical interpretation that is accomplished
using various approaches in which words, phrases, verses,
and sections of biblical texts are subjected to critical analysis.
Practitioners of biblical exegesis ask questions of the *texts* to
understand the *context* (the surrounding circumstances and
situations) of a biblical passage. They try to determine who
wrote the texts, why they wrote them, what was happening
in the communities and cultures in which the texts originated,
when the texts were written, and how the language the writers used in the texts conveys meaning. Biblical exegetes believe that texts should not be interpreted without taking into
account their literary, social, and historical contexts.

A contemporary example of the importance of context
can be found in the case of Shirley Sherrod, former Georgia
state director of Rural Development for the United States
Department of Agriculture. In July 2010 Sherrod was forced
to resign her position when a blogger released a video clip
that captured her saying that she, an African American
woman, had not given a white farmer all the help to save
his farm that she could have. After administration officials
reviewed the entire tape *in context*, they found that Sherrod *did* state that she had not given that white farmer the

full force of her help—at first. However, Sherrod went on to explain that when she later found out that the attorney to whom she had referred the white farmer was unhelpful, she diligently searched for another attorney. She found an attorney for the farmer who helped him save his family's farm. She confessed that working with the white farmer heightened her awareness of the need to help all poor people regardless of their race.[3] The administration subsequently apologized for the mistake.

Since the questions biblical exegetes ask of the Bible are the same questions that academics raise of secular texts, some Christians reject their methods. Kenyon and many other evangelicals of his day felt the Bible should never be treated like a secular document. Therefore, Kenyon rejected biblical exegesis. In doing so, he and other evangelicals were attempting to defend the Bible from being assaulted by outsiders whom they felt were decidedly unchristian.[4] However, he also rejected the tendency of orthodox[5] leaders and theologians to uncritically defend their historic creeds and particular denominational understandings of Scripture. Kenyon chose instead to emphasize holiness and personal experience with the Holy Spirit.[6]

PROOF TEXTING

Kenyon used two primary approaches to biblical interpretation: proof texting and typology. Kenyon was proof texting when he chose a theme for a sermon or lesson and then used isolated verses to support his theme. Kenyon had a very literal view of Scripture. He believed the Bible meant exactly what it said (or should be understood exactly the way it was read), and there was no need for observing the context—literary or historical and cultural. Another way of explaining Kenyon's perspective is that he believed the Bible was God's propositional revelation, which God supernaturally communicated to chosen people in the form of "cognitive truths."[7]

In propositional revelation, every sentence of the Bible is a divinely inspired truth and part of God's redemptive plan for humanity, which begins in Genesis and culminates in the person and work of Jesus Christ. No sentence in the Bible contradicts any other sentence. Kenyon's belief that the Bible is God's propositional revelation explains why he chose themes for his preaching and teaching and then found verses that contained words or phrases related to his theme to support his main points. However, as with much literal interpretation, Kenyon's use of Scripture often did not support his contentions when they were read in context. For example, to substantiate his claim that believers were overcomers of the world and thereby entitled to prosperity in all things, Kenyon cited 1 John 5:4-5 as evidence: "For whatsoever is born of God overcometh the world: and this is the victory that overcometh the world, even our faith. Who is he that overcometh the world, but he that believeth that Jesus is the Son of God?" (KJV).

By reading further in 1 John 2:15-16, we discover that by the phrase "overcoming the world," the writer meant resisting such temptations or shortcomings as "lust of the flesh," "lust of the eyes," and "pride of life." In the text, the writer was attempting to convince believers that they could be victorious over all sin through Jesus Christ. Therefore, Kenyon's belief that "overcoming the world" meant not being in lack or in poverty is not supported by the text itself.

TYPOLOGY

Kenyon also used typology, the study of types or symbols. He was interpreting typologically when he identified people and objects in the Old Testament with Christ. Kenyon read the entire Bible as a revelation of the redemptive work of God, which began after the fall of Adam and culminated with the death, burial, and resurrection of Christ and the gifting of the Holy Spirit.

An example of Kenyon's use of typology as interpretive method can be found in his interpretation of Exodus 25:31: "And thou shalt make a candlestick of pure gold: of beaten work shall the candlestick be made: his shaft, and his branches, his bowls, his knops, and his flowers, shall be of the same" (KJV). For Kenyon, the golden candlestick was a symbol of the union of Christ with his body, the church.[8] He also believed that the author of Exodus used "branches" as a foreshadowing of Christ's words in John 15:5, "I am the vine, ye are the branches" (KJV). For Kenyon, though God desired a dwelling place in the midst of Israel and had them construct the sanctuary to fulfill that desire, Christ fulfilled God's desire to dwell among the people. As a result, Kenyon believed the Exodus passage symbolized humanity's union with Christ, made through Christ's death, burial, and resurrection.

By interpreting Exodus 25:31 typologically, Kenyon ignored the wondrous work God was doing among the Israelites. In fact, he asserted that God had never actually dwelled among the people of Israel. However, when we read the book of Exodus, we see over and over again that God *was* among the people of Israel. God brought them out of Egypt, slavery, and bondage while performing miracle after miracle on their behalf. God commanded Moses to consecrate the people at Mount Sinai (Exodus 19:9-15) and gave the Israelites laws by which to govern their lives (Exodus 19–23). God instructed them to build a tabernacle so they would be reminded of God's presence among them (Exodus 25).

By turning all attention toward Christ and what God is doing in the New Testament, typological interpreters such as Kenyon ignore what God was doing among the people in the Old Testament in general and what God was doing in these verses in particular. God had instructed the people of Israel to build a tabernacle in which the Spirit of God would dwell. The lampstand would be just one of the articles God instructed the people to make for the tabernacle. Together, all of the items would create a sacred space even as the Israelites journeyed to the Promised Land.

Whereas Kenyon rejected all biblical exegesis as a secular tool inappropriate for sacred Scripture, today's Word of Faith preachers who are trained at Rhema Bible Training Center in Broken Arrow, Oklahoma, are taught how to do some exegetical work by always observing the context of Scripture passages. However, before they read or attempt to interpret any biblical text, they are taught to pray for guidance and to listen for the voice of the Holy Spirit as they seek meaning.

By observing the context, students learn that they should ask questions about the setting and time frame in which a book was written and who is speaking in the text (God or humans). To answer questions that arise when they observe the context, students are taught to use tools of biblical interpretation, such as Bible dictionaries, atlases, handbooks, commentaries, and concordances. While, on the one hand, students are trained to raise questions of texts and use resources to find answers, they are also taught to allow the Bible to interpret itself (i.e., some texts in the Bible can help to interpret other parts) and not to overspiritualize everything (the passages mean exactly what they say).

In the course for ministry leaders, students learn that the Bible is not just any ancient text. The Bible holds the answers to each student's problems and serves as a handbook for daily living for all Christians.[9] They are taught that the predominant theme that permeates all Scripture (both the Old and New Testaments) is "the redemption of mankind through a divinely appointed Savior."[10] They are taught that biblical writers were each assigned by God to write different portions of biblical text. However, only God understood the complete plan of redemption and the role that each writer would play in the redemptive drama that unfolded over the centuries.[11]

For example, proof that the Bible is the word of God can be found in the word of God itself in texts such as 2 Timothy 3:16.[12] As we already observed, Jesse Duplantis and other

Word of Faith preachers seize upon this verse as foundational to their literal view of the Bible. When Duplantis stated, "Scripture . . . comes from the lips of God," he was asserting that every word of the Bible as we know it today was dictated to human authors by God. Duplantis was also claiming that 2 Timothy 3:16 provided biblical proof that his assertion was correct.

Duplantis's view of Scripture exceeds the teachings students receive at Rhema. Students at Rhema receive some encouragement to consult nonbiblical sources to interpret texts. However, they are also taught that the Bible should not be treated like any other secular book because it is sacred, having been written by people who were inspired by God. Duplantis contends that the Bible was dictated by God.

Sifting the Wheat from the Chaff

The reverence that Rhema students hold for the Bible is instructive. They are constantly aware that the Bible is sacred and can and does serve as a guide for those who are trying to live Christian lives. Every Christian needs to be reminded to pray before interpreting the Bible. When we read the Bible, we are often trying to understand not just what the text meant to the people in the ancient world but what the text means for our world, for our communities, for our families, and for us as individuals. Therefore, allowing the Holy Spirit to guide the interpretive process is important.

In addition, as students are taught at Rhema, there are some verses in the Bible that seem to mean exactly what they say. For example, the Golden Rule of Matthew 7:12, "In everything do to others as you would have them do to you; for this is the law and the prophets," seems to need no further explanation. The verse does not seem to need interpretation until or unless one raises questions about what followers of Christ are supposed "to do." What Christians do in their daily lives (and therefore expect others to do to them) is guided by their interpretations of the Bible. Even in this seemingly straightforward verse, meaning relies on underlying assumptions in the minds of interpreters about what being Christian actually means.

Kenyon and the evangelicals of his day did not so much defend the Bible from biblical exegesis as they rejected exegesis outright. Unlike the biblical exegetes, Kenyon viewed the Bible as propositional revelation in which every sentence of the Bible stands on its own as a divinely imparted truth. This view, however, has its limitations. If Kenyon were correct, there are a lot of verses that defy explanation.

For instance, how should verses such as 1 Timothy 2:15 be interpreted: "Notwithstanding she shall be saved in childbearing, if they continue in faith and charity and holiness with sobriety" (KJV)? The biblical writer seems to be saying that women have to earn their salvation through bearing children and doing other good works. If that is true, then this verse plainly contradicts Ephesians 2:8-9, which reads: "For by grace are ye saved through faith; and that not of yourselves: it is the gift of God: not of works, lest any man should boast" (KJV). The writer of Ephesians argued strenuously that neither men nor women had to earn salvation. Salvation was not granted because of human works. All women and men had to do to receive salvation was ask God. That means that women did not have to bear children or be modest, holy, faithful, or loving to be saved. All they had to do was ask God and God would freely grant them salvation.

When verses of the Bible are interpreted without consideration of the texts that surround them and without attempting to understand who wrote the texts, why they were written, and how the writers used language in the texts to convey meaning, the texts can be made to mean almost anything. For years, verses such as Deuteronomy 15:12-15, Ephesians 6:9, and Colossians 4:1 were used to justify the enslavement of Africans in North America. After all, according to Ephesians 6:9, slaves were to obey their masters in the same ways they were to obey Christ, with fear and trembling, singleness of heart, and enthusiasm. By using isolated Scriptures to justify human enslavement, slave owners told slaves that it was God's will for them to be slaves. Because the Bible was considered incontrovertible proof of God's will, slave traders and slave owners used the existence of the practice of slavery in the Bible as proof that slavery was sanctioned by God. They argued that if the Bible offered no critique of slavery, then slavery was sanctioned by God. If slavery was sanctioned by God, slavery was not just sanctioned for ancient Israel and the first-century Roman Empire, but also for seventeenth, eighteenth, and early nineteenth-century North America.

Interpretation of biblical texts out of context has been used, and is still being used, to deny the ordination of women (1 Corinthians 14:34) and justify their subjugation to male authority (Ephesians 5:22-23). It has been used to deny the legality of interracial marriage (Genesis 28:1) and support separation of the races (Acts 17:24-26). It has been used to justify the annihilation of indigenous people all over the world (Joshua 1:3) and the murder of gays and lesbians (Leviticus 20:13). Literal interpretation of the Bible has been and continues to be a dangerous practice. By asserting that the Bible is the dictated word of God and that every sentence in it reflects the will of God without regard to context, there is no limit to the atrocities that the Bible can be made to condone.

Typological interpretation renders the audience for which the biblical author was writing virtually irrelevant by focusing instead on the implications of the text for God's larger redemptive work in Christ. When typological interpretation is used, hearers may be robbed of the benefit of seeing God's grace and mercy at work in the lives of people who often behaved just like them (being disobedient) or found themselves in similar situations (being oppressed or not understanding God's will for their lives).

Biblical exegesis regards biblical texts as products of their particular cultures that reflected the social mores of their day.

However, biblical exegetes believe that particular practices or ways of being that were common in the Old and New Testaments were not necessarily God's will for the people of God then nor are they necessarily God's will for our lives today.

Prosperity preachers use many passages of the Bible to support their beliefs that God wants all believers to be rich and have good physical health. As we will see in the next chapter, they also use the doctrine of the divine economy as part of their argument.

NOTES

1. Jesse Duplantis is the founder of Jesse Duplantis Ministries, headquartered in Destrehan, Louisiana. The ministry also has offices in the United Kingdom and Australia. Duplantis's sermons are broadcast on television networks around the world. He is widely known for his sense of humor. Biography, Jesse Duplantis Ministries, January 22, 2010, http://www.jdm.org/jdmDefault.aspx?tabindex=-1&tabID=36 (accessed December 13, 2011).

2. E. W. Kenyon, *Identification: A Romance in Redemption* (Lynnwood, WA: Kenyon's Gospel Publishing Society, 1941), 51–52.

3. Shirley Sherrod, Shirley Sherrod: The Full Video, YouTube, October 4, 2010, http://www.youtube.com/watch?v=E9NcCa_KjXk (accessed December 13, 2011).

4. Alister McGrath, *A Passion for Truth: The Intellectual Coherence of Evangelicalism* (Downers Grove, IL: InterVarsity, 1996), 59.

5. Kenyon uses the term *orthodox* to refer to those who espouse a literal approach to the Bible and reject higher criticism and its intellectual approach to interpretation.

6. Ibid.

7. Carl Ferdinand Howard Henry, *God, Revelation, and Authority*, 6 vols. (Wheaton, IL: Crossway, 1999), 456.

8. E. W. Kenyon, *The Bible in Light of Our Redemption: Basic Bible Course* (Old Tappan, NJ: Revell, 1969), 107–8.

9. Ibid., 36.

10. Myer Pearlman, *Seeing the Story of the Bible* (Springfield, MO: Gospel, 1930), 9.

11. Ibid., 12.

12. Ibid., 59. Second Timothy 3:16 reads, "All scripture is given by inspiration of God, and is profitable for doctrine, for reproof, for correction, for instruction in righteousness" (KJV).

CHAPTER 3

The World's Economy Is Not Your Economy

In a sermon titled "No More Toil," Bill Winston,[1] founder of the nineteen-thousand-member Living Word Christian Center in Oak Park, Illinois, taught his congregation that they needed to switch systems.[2] Instead of relying on the world's economic system to meet their economic needs, they needed to start believing in God's system. "Your days of working for a paycheck are over," stated Winston.

By this he did not mean that his hearers did not need to work. Rather, he meant that they no longer needed to rely on their paychecks to support their standards of living. If they had faith in God, they would believe that by sowing into the kingdom of God (i.e., giving money to churches and people to whom God directed them to give), God would make them wealthy. Winston told a story about how he and his wife had approached purchasing a home. After they had looked for some time, the Holy Spirit told Winston to ask his wife, Veronica, which house she liked. When he asked, she looked at him and said, "You mean which house we can *afford*." "No," he said, "which house you *like*."

Winston pointed out to the congregation that his wife, like everyone else, had been programmed to work within the world's system, wherein people who want to buy a house sit down with a mortgage broker to determine whether they can qualify for a home loan. The mortgage broker also determines a loan amount for which prospective home buyers qualify based on income and assets. "We are not part of that system anymore," Winston declared. He was operating out of another kingdom that had different rules. The other kingdom was not like the toil-based system that Satan constructed.

So Veronica told her husband what house she liked best. They prayed about it, and God told them to go and point at the house. They went to the house, pointed at it, and commanded the house to sell to them. After a series of miracles, they bought the house.

To continue to make his case for the validity of God's economic system, Winston tried to anticipate the criticisms of skeptics. Knowing that some of his hearers would think pointing at a house was silly, he shared a story about a Christian man in Port-au-Prince, Haiti, who spoke to a tree being used by voodoo witch doctors. After the man spoke to the tree and cursed it, the tree dried up. If the man could speak to a tree and cause it to dry up, Winston stated, there was no reason why anyone could not speak to a house (or some issue) and cause circumstances to work in their favor.

To justify his teaching biblically, Winston cited John 6:1-14, in which Jesus fed the multitude with two fish and five loaves of bread. Winston told his hearers that on that occasion Jesus was teaching the disciples how to meet a need without toil or hard labor. God led Jesus to feed the multitude. However, they were in a place that made feeding them difficult to do. According to Winston, when Philip told Jesus that six months' worth of wages would not be enough money to buy food to give each person in the crowd even a little bit, the disciple was operating in the world's system. Philip believed only what he saw. Jesus, however, was operating in another system. Winston declared that he wanted his hearers to trust completely in God's system rather in Satan's system, the system of the world. He told his hearers that companies in the world come and go, but God's kingdom would be around when everything else is gone.

Although Winston did not "sow seed" to obtain the house, his story illustrated the practical applications of the divine economy. In a broad sense, the divine economy is described as the realm in which God blesses people (usually financially) based on their faith. Prosperity preachers reference other biblical texts to support their belief that God's economy works very differently than the world's economy.

Heirs according to the Promise

God's divine economy operates by faith in God's will and ability to keep all of the promises given in the Bible. Prosperity preachers teach their followers that if God made a promise, then God will keep it—even if keeping it seems impossible by human standards. God will keep God's promises because God is faithful and able to do all things.

According to Word of Faith theology, Christians are heirs to the promise God made to Abraham (then Abram) and his seed. Evidence that Christians are heirs is found in Galatians 3:28-29: "There is neither Jew nor Greek, there is neither bond nor free, there is neither male nor female: for ye are all one in Christ Jesus. And if ye be Christ's, then are ye Abraham's seed, and heirs according to the promise" (KJV).

God made a covenant with Abram in Genesis 17. In the covenant, God promised to bless Abram by making him the ancestor of many nations. Kings would be among his many descendants. God also promised to be faithful to Abram and his offspring and to give him land. In return for God's everlasting faithfulness, God required obedience and male circumcision. Circumcision was a physical symbol of the covenant between Abram and his descendants that was to be everlasting.

However, although Galatians refers to this Abrahamic promise, Word of Faith preachers teach their followers that the promises God made in the Mosaic law are also part of believers' inheritances. For example, Kenyon taught his followers that the law was given to the people already in covenant with God in order to provide concrete guidelines about how they should live their daily lives.[3] He also taught that the curse of the law was overcome by the new covenant God established with humanity through Jesus. The new covenant permanently restored the relationship between God and humanity that Adam's sin had broken. As a result, all the promises that God made to Abraham are promises God has made to all followers of Christ.

Kenyon wrote that the new covenant entitle believers to certain rights and privileges that, when claimed and acted upon, allow believers to live lives of victory and success instead of lives of defeat and failure. Included in the law are promises to bless the people of Israel if they obeyed God's ordinances. For example, in Deuteronomy 7:12-15, God promised to love, bless, and multiply the Israelites; to bless the fruit of the ground including grain, wine, and oil; to bless their cattle and flock in the land God gave them; and to keep them free of sickness and disease. Another favorite is Deuteronomy 28:13, where God promised to make the Israelites the head and not the tail. In other words, they would be rulers rather than the ruled.

The law of Moses is comprehensive. In addition to all the blessings of God that were contingent on obedience, there were also curses of God that were the consequences of disobedience. For example, in Deuteronomy 28:15-19 God promised to curse the land, flocks, progeny, crops, and general lives of those who did not observe all of God's commandments.

Yet prosperity preachers do not subscribe to the law in detail. They teach adherents that Jesus came to fulfill the law, yet they pick and choose parts of the law to claim as applicable to Christians today. Can prosperity theology have it both ways? Before commenting on Bill Winston's sermon and faith teachings about God's promises and the law, let's examine how some prosperity preachers have responded to the global economic crisis.

Prosperity Gospel and the Global Economic Crisis

Purveyors of prosperity theology fully understood the gravity of the global economic crisis and openly acknowledged that many of their hearers were impacted by it. The titles of hundreds of sermons from 2008 through 2010 indicated that preachers were attempting to address the concerns of their followers. However, while they acknowledged the conditions of the secular world, they reminded their hearers of the dualistic nature of their Christian existence by saying repeatedly, "The world's recession is not your recession." They told their followers that God has promised to supply all of their needs according to God's riches in Christ Jesus (Philippians 4:19). Therefore, even if things seem momentarily bleak, God would not only give them what they needed, but would bless them with the desires of their hearts. To receive the blessings of God, believers must be faithful to God in every way. Being faithful includes giving their tithes and offerings.

With so much preaching in prosperity circles about the need to give tithes and offerings even in (or especially in) the time of economic crisis, it was no wonder that large Word of Faith conferences experienced record-breaking financial giving during the crisis. Gloria Copeland, wife and ministry partner of Kenneth Copeland,[4] stated in August 2009 that the recession had no power over the church. She made this comment just after her husband had announced that the conference receipts had exceeded budgeted expectations by $556,654. Total offerings on the sixth and last day of the conference totaled $1,227,000, with at least one offering remaining to be collected. When asked if they would still be collecting the offering since the conference was already over budget, Copeland said, "Are you kidding me? Absolutely so!" He explained that since all of the conference expenses had been paid in advance, all of the offerings (all $1,227,000) would go to outreach. In addition, Kenneth Copeland claimed that God told him (in relation to the tremendous debt being accumulated by the United States government), "If you will stir up your faith and you get the body of Christ stirred up about it, I'll give you the money and you can pay off the government's debt. And when you do, you will own it."[5] Copeland obviously believes that with God all things are possible.

George Pearsons, son-in-law of Kenneth and Gloria Copeland, compared the global economic crisis to the time of famine in Genesis 26. He said that for people who do not know God and do not understand their covenant, the economic crisis that began in 2008 is a serious and frightful time. Some people had committed suicide while others are afraid that everything they had worked for all their lives is going to be lost. However, when there was famine in the land in Isaac's day, he did not just survive, he thrived. Therefore, as the seed of Abraham, believers can thrive during the economic crisis. Isaac, said Pearsons, was the richest man in the world. Christians are descendants of that seed. In order to thrive, Christians continually need to do what Isaac had done. By examining Isaac's behavior during the famine, believers can understand the importance of obeying God, sowing seed and tithing, and attending church.

Pearsons used Zechariah 8:11-13 to demonstrate the need for obedience.

> But now I will not be unto the residue of this people as in the former days, saith the LORD of hosts. For the seed shall be prosperous; the vine shall give her fruit, and the ground shall give her increase, and the heavens shall give their dew; and I will cause the remnant of this people to possess all these things. And it shall come to pass, that as ye were a curse among the heathen,

O house of Judah, and house of Israel; so will I save you, and ye
shall be a blessing: fear not, but let your hands be strong. (KJV)

In the text, God promised to bless the people but demanded obedience in return. Pearsons contended that obedience is the key to success in time of famine. Believers need to do what God tells them to do and be where God tells them to be.

In the biblical text, Isaac sowed and received a hundred-fold return for his seed. Pearsons emphasized that having such bountiful yield in Gerar was miraculous. The area was not very fertile. Even when there was no famine, the most fertile parts of the country yielded only a 25 to 50 percent return on their crops. Just as Isaac's blessings defied the reality of his environment, Pearsons declared, the blessings God has in store for Christians will not be limited by the economic crisis or famine around them. Christians operate on a different level. They live and reign as kings and priests. They are the seed of Abraham. As a result, the same blessings that God promised and delivered to Isaac are available to all Christians.

Genesis 26 reported that Isaac became a very wealthy man. And Pearsons declared that Isaac paid tithes on all of his possessions. He admitted that though not explicitly stated in the text, he believes that Isaac tithed because Abraham tithed (Genesis 14:20). Isaac learned obedience to God from his father. Just as God blessed Isaac's obedience, God will also bless believers who demonstrate obedience to God by tithing.

Pearsons also told his hearers that the period of economic crisis is not a time to stop attending church. They should not just watch a preacher on television or via the internet. Though God grants grace for people who cannot come to church and watch services from home, those who can attend need to be present in the house of the Lord. He cited Psalm 92:12-13 to remind listeners that those who are planted in the house of the Lord flourish. He defined flourishing as increasing in wealth and honor. The Hebrew term for flourish, *parach*, actually means to bud, sprout, bloom, or blossom.

The goal of Pearson's sermon was to provide encouragement and hope to the congregation during the time of crisis. Based on the congregation's amen's and applause during his sermon, he succeeded.

Sifting the Wheat from the Chaff

One of the gifts that prosperity theology brings to Christianity and the world is an unwavering faith in God's ability to do the seemingly impossible. Steadfast and resolute faith is a central tenet of Word of Faith theology and is communicated in every Word of Faith sermon. In other spheres of Christianity, the omnipotence of God is not always as revered or celebrated.

While faith in the power of God is highly valued in Word of Faith preaching, critical consideration of sermons from Winston and others raise a variety of issues and concerns. Let's focus here on Winston's divine economy.

By telling his hearers that their days of working for a paycheck were over, Winston was telling his hearers to ignore the concrete reality that earning a particular income creates. In the world, most people center their lives on the income they earn. They buy or rent homes that they can afford with their salaries. They spend money on food, clothes, cars, entertainment, and other essential and nonessential items based on their incomes. Creating a life based on income is also known as living within one's means—means that are gifts of God. Everything we have and everything we are (the best of what we are) are gifts of God. So when prosperity theology conceives of the world in dualistic terms, God and the human world being two separate entities, they are shortchanging the God of all creation whom they say they revere. God does not only operate in the sphere of the divine economy. God is God of all.

Believing that God has the ability to affect situations that are beyond our control can be a positive attribute. However, intentionally creating situations "by faith" in which God must intervene in an ongoing way is irresponsible. For example, sometimes people are denied loans to buy houses they *can* afford simply because of where they live (redlining) or on the basis of race or ethnicity (racism and ethnocentricism). Praying for God to intervene in such situations and acting to change the legality of this type of discrimination demonstrates faith. However, there are also times when people pray for God to help them obtain loans for homes they know they cannot actually afford. This is irresponsible. Is it also putting God to the test?

In Matthew 4:7 Satan tempted Jesus in the desert. He tried to get Jesus to throw himself off of the pinnacle of the temple and expect angels to catch him before he fell to his death. Jesus responded, "It is written again, 'Thou shalt not tempt the Lord thy God'" (KJV), or put God to the test. When Jesus used these words, he was referring to Exodus 17 when the Israelites complained to Moses in the wilderness that there was no water to drink. Throughout their journey, God had met their needs without fail. Yet the Israelites somehow failed to believe God's faithfulness would continue. When Jesus quoted this Scripture, he seemed to be telling Satan that, while God was faithful and would meet his needs, he would not knowingly create a situation wherein a miraculous act of God was his only hope of escape.

Assuming a mortgage that one cannot afford willingly and knowingly creates a situation in which God's miraculous and ongoing intervention is the only hope of maintaining it. Is that not the type of act Jesus refused to perform? As followers of Christ, should we not refuse to put God to the test?

Through his personal testimony, Winston encouraged hearers to buy the houses they wanted versus the ones they could afford. Winston shared his testimony as evidence of the validity of the divine economy in which the sacred economy of God is premised over the secular economy of the world. In the divine economy, one needs only to have faith that God can do all things and sow seeds of faith to reap bountiful harvests. Bountiful harvests can include a home.

Several articles have been written and news stories have been published linking prosperity theology to the mortgage crisis. In one documentary, a woman named Cynthia Simons from Compton, California, thought her prayers were being answered when a mortgage broker from her church found her a house in safe neighborhood.[6] Simons said that one Sunday the broker came to her church and said, "Hallelujah, thank you, Jesus, you got the loan." With that news, she thought she was the beneficiary of a miracle. Her family would be able to move out of a bad neighborhood into the home of their dreams. The broker offered her a five-year adjustable rate mortgage that she said Cynthia could refinance in five years. However, by the time Cynthia was ready to refinance, the housing market had crashed and she could not find another loan. The mortgage payment increased tremendously, and she could not pay. When she was interviewed in 2009, she was certain her home would go into foreclosure at any time. She realized that signing papers for a loan she did not understand was not a miracle; it was bad judgment.

Banks like Wells Fargo partnered with pastors, especially those who taught prosperity theology, to conduct wealth-building seminars in their churches. The purpose of the seminars was to "dazzle the participants with the possibility of a new house."[7] Wells Fargo donated $350 to the churches or to any charities the pastors chose for every loan made to members. Rather than telling the ministers that their parishioners would be signing papers for subprime loans, bank representatives told them that their members would be able to achieve the American dream of home ownership. Churches in low income areas in general, and prosperity preaching churches in particular, were easy targets for predatory lending.[8] Neither the pastors nor the members asked too many questions. They believed God was working in their favor.

While many of the pastors who worked with banks to provide their members access to mortgage loans may have been earnest and sincere, they were not the ones who became homeless when the mortgages were foreclosed. In addition to being evicted from their homes and having their credit damaged, members may have been left with a sense of shame, regret, and perhaps even a crisis of faith. Cynthia Simons realized that she exercised poor judgment by signing a loan without reading the fine print. Reading her loan documentation could have enabled Cynthia to make an informed decision about whether to buy that particular home, buy a more affordable home, or wait to purchase a home until she had saved additional funds. Making informed decisions goes hand in hand with godly blessings. Being able to find a home that one likes and can afford is a blessing. Having the mental ability to weigh the merits of viable loan options is a blessing. Being able to review and improve one's credit to qualify for better loan terms is a blessing. Truly understanding the terms of a loan is a blessing. Having a job that provides a regular income so one can qualify for a mortgage is a blessing.

The dualistic nature of prosperity preaching encourages believers to ignore important details that expose them to risks they otherwise could avoid if they would realize that God can be in the details. Since prosperity preachers teach their congregants that material prosperity and good physical health are the right of every Christian, when followers do not realize the material blessings prosperity preachers assert they should, preachers place the blame squarely on the shoulders of the people. Preachers tell followers they failed because they did not have enough faith, they did not sow enough seeds, their lives were too tainted by sin, or they did not follow all the steps the preachers said they should. Any preacher who makes unfounded promises and then blames followers for the failure of those promises to materialize is engaging in ungodly preaching.

Dualism is evident in Winston's discussion of John 6:1-14. Winston interpreted the miracle of Jesus feeding the multitude as a lesson about the need to trust in God versus trusting in the world. That is one interpretation. Another interpretation is that Jesus saw a need. People had been listening faithfully and were hungry. There was little food and no place nearby for the crowd to go to be fed. Jesus did not perform the miracle simply to demonstrate the power of God at work in him, although he did accomplish that. Jesus performed the miracle to fulfill a real need. God will meet human needs. When sufficient resources are not available to meet our human needs, God will provide.

The need for believers to be obedient to God is another recurring theme in prosperity preaching. The preachers often tell their followers that Christianity is not about reasoning or questioning God's word. If believers obey God, they will prosper. However, prosperity preachers teach their followers that obeying God means being obedient to the word of God (the Bible), which preachers interpret in their preaching. In this interpretive process, God's authority, biblical authority, and pastoral authority are intermingled. Is every interpretation of the Bible God's word? Is every preacher faithful to the word of God? What happens if or when the teachings of the preacher are not godly?

The unquestioned obedience that prosperity preachers espouse does not take into account human fallibility. No matter how godly preachers may be, they are not God. Preachers are human, with shortcomings and a variety of worldviews, allegiances, and alliances that influence the ways they interpret the Bible. In addition, by declaring reason to be an enemy of faith, prosperity preachers fail to acknowledge that knowledge and the ability to think critically are also gifts of God. If their teachings are biblically sound, preachers should not feel threatened by reason.

Having faith in God and having the ability to reason and think critically about one's faith should not be mutually exclusive endeavors. God is the giver of the mind and all the gifts and talents that emerge from its use and engagement. Though humans have the potential to use their gifts and talents to engage in sin, those same gifts and skills offer believers the ability and unlimited opportunities to glorify God. To limit critical engagement because of fear of sin or error also limits the possibilities of being a blessing to others.

Prosperity preachers teach their followers that God wants all believers to be rich. Therefore, they certainly could not then teach that the central figure of the Gospels is poor. That is what we will explore in chapter 4.

NOTES

1. Bill Winston founded Living Word Christian Center in 1989 with fewer than fifty members. With more than nineteen thousand members today, the church also operates a Bible training school and a Christian academy, as well as two shopping malls in the Forest Park, Illinois, area. First lady Veronica Winston oversees the prayer ministry and the women's ministry. "History," Living Word Christian Center, www.billwinston.org/bwm_main.aspx?id=34 (accessed January 20, 2010).

2. Bill Winston, "No More Toil," Bill Winston Minstries, www.billwinston.org/bwm_main.aspx?id=49 (accessed May 3, 2010).

3. E. W. Kenyon, *Basic Bible Course: The Bible in the Light of Our Redemption* (Lynnwood, WA: Kenyon's Gospel Publishing Society, 1999), 98–99.

4. Kenneth Copeland is the founder and CEO of Kenneth Copeland Ministries, based in Fort Worth, Texas.

5. Kenneth Copeland, "Saturday, August 8, 2009," 2009 Kenneth Copeland Ministries Events Video Podcast, iTunes, downloaded July 12, 2010.

6. "House of Cards," CNBC, http://www.cnbc.com/id/15840232?video=1145392808&play=1 (accessed September 14, 2009).

7. Hanna Rosin, "Did Christianity Cause the Mortgage Crisis?" *Atlantic*, December, 2009: www.theatlantic.com/magazine/archive/2009/12/did-christianity-cause-the-crash/7764/2 (accessed December 13, 2011).

8. Ibid.

CHAPTER 4

Poverty Is a Curse, and Jesus Was Not Poor

To the more than twenty-five thousand people who attended a Full Gospel Church conference in New Orleans in 2004, Leroy Thompson,[1] pastor of the seventeen-hundred member Word of Life Christian Center in Darrow, Louisiana, was the bearer of very good news. In a message titled "Breaking the Generational Curse of Poverty," Thompson told the congregation that Christians have been redeemed from the curse of poverty.[2] To support his contention that poverty is a curse, Thompson cited Galatians 3:13-14: "Christ hath redeemed us from the curse of the law, being made a curse for us: for it is written, Cursed is every one that hangeth on a tree: that the blessing of Abraham might come on the Gentiles through Jesus Christ; that we might receive the promise of the Spirit through faith" (KJV).

Thompson, like other Word of Faith preachers, teaches his congregation that the blessings of Abraham are the inheritance of all Christians. The promises of God found in the law are also part of the inheritance given to Christians by God. God promised to bless the people of God who are obedient and curse the ones who are not. Part of the curse for

46

disobedience is poverty. Since prosperity preachers teach that poverty is a curse, they cannot subscribe to the traditional Christian belief that Jesus was impoverished. So what do they do with Jesus?

Jesus Was Not Poor

Since prosperity preachers contend that poverty is a curse, they must argue that the central figure of the gospel, Jesus Christ himself, was not poor. Without addressing Jesus' socioeconomic status, they would have no hope of being taken seriously. To substantiate their teachings, they use circumstantial evidence. For example, in one sermon, Creflo Dollar (founder and senior pastor of World Changers Church International in College Park, Georgia) taught his listeners that Jesus was not poor, using as proof the facts that (1) Jesus had a treasurer and (2) John's disciples were so impressed by his living situation that they did not return to their master.

> Jesus was not poor. He had so much money that he needed a treasurer to take care of everything. He ate whatever he wanted and whenever he desired it. He lived in a place that commanded envy, because John's disciples who went to see where he lived never returned to their master. They remained with Jesus. If you walk in poverty, then you don't look like Jesus. And we are representations of Jesus. So we should be an expression of Jesus to the world the same way Jesus was to the Father.[3]

Although Dollar did not cite chapter and verse, he was referencing the occasion in John 1:39 when two of John's disciples followed Jesus and asked him where he was staying. In this text, Jesus advised the disciples to "come and see" (KJV) where he was living. The disciples followed him and stayed with him for the rest of the day. Dollar proclaimed that since the disciples stayed with Jesus the entire day, his house must have been very nice. Dollar did not seem to consider the possibility that the disciples stayed with Jesus because they were being blessed by his teachings or because the presence of the Spirit of God dwelled within and around him.

Dollar also said that the existence of a treasurer (Judas; see John 12:6) among Jesus' disciples was evidence of Jesus' wealth. His logic was that if Jesus did not have much money, he would not have needed a treasurer.

In another sermon, Dollar referred to the circumstances of Jesus' birth as proof that he was not poor:

> See, because some people thought, "Oh, poor Mary and Joseph riding on their donkey into Bethlehem." What you don't understand is that very few people owned donkeys to ride on. That was a Cadillac in that day, brother. Joseph wasn't poor. Mary wasn't poor. Somebody said, "What do you mean? How do you know that they were not poor?" You remember those three wise men God sent to him [Jesus]? You need to read it again to see what they brought them. [By the] time Jesus was born, man, God had wealth funneled into his way. Ha, ha, glory to God. Somebody said, "All right, all right, if he's not poor, then how come they stayed in a little barn?" You know, how come they couldn't rent a room? 'Cause they were all filled up. Man's fortunate that he didn't buy them out that night.[4]

Sifting the Wheat from the Chaff

Dollar's contention that Judas served as treasurer is consistent with Scripture. However, in John 12:6 and 13:29 readers discover that Judas served as the treasurer, or keeper of "the common purse," for all of the disciples, not just for Jesus. Therefore, the need for someone to keep the purse may not have been a result of there being so *much* money, but simply as a way of centralizing the financial resources and developing accountability.

The donkey of John 12:12-15 was more likely akin to a Ford Fiesta than to a Cadillac. In Zechariah 9:9 the prophet foretold the coming of a humble ruler riding a donkey, a ruler who would shun the usual royal trappings of horses and chariots. The royal trappings of chariots and horses evolved under the leadership of King Solomon. Solomon's father David had been much more modest. In 1 Kings 1:33 when David wanted to declare to all of Israel that Solomon was the heir to the throne, he had Solomon ride his mule, which is a cross between a male donkey and a mare or female horse. However, after Solomon became king, he upgraded the royal transportation by developing a fleet of horses and chariots (1 Kings 10:26). In Zechariah and in John's Gospel, the donkey represents peace and humility, whereas horses and chariots represent war and "elitism."[5] Therefore, the Cadillacs of Jesus' day would have been horses and chariots rather than the donkeys.

The "inn" of Luke 2:7 was likely a *guest room* in a house. In Luke the writer used the term *kataluma* to refer to a guest room or house. When the writer referred to a commercial inn, he used the term *pandocheion* (10:34).[6] In addition, scholars argue that it is unlikely there were any commercial inns in Bethlehem, because it was not connected to any of the major roadways.

The "manger" of Luke 2:7 was commonly found built into the floor of peasant homes in ancient Palestine, which further supports the idea that Jesus' parents were housed by fellow peasants and not seeking accommodations in a prestigious hotel. The standard peasant home consisted of a living area for the family and a small area roughly four feet lower where livestock could be sheltered at night—with access to the in-floor manger.[7]

Shepherds were declared unclean by many rabbis.[8] Their profession cast them at the bottom of the social ladder. Shepherds were not welcomed in many places.[9] If Jesus had been of a high socioeconomic status, shepherds would not have been allowed to visit him. The magi or wise men did visit Jesus, giving him gold, frankincense, and myrrh. However, the text does not reveal how much of the treasure the wise men left. Nor does either text indicate how many wise men were there. And contrary to Dollar's preaching, neither Matthew nor Luke mentions that Mary and Joseph rode into Bethlehem on a donkey. On the basis of Matthew and Luke and sociohistorical information about Palestine in the first century, Joseph and Mary were not rich. They were peasants.[10]

Dollar argued that people who walked in poverty did not look like Jesus. But by painting Jesus as a person of a higher socioeconomic class, Dollar alienates some people from the one who came to save all. In first-century Judaism, the poor were people who owned no land and had few financial resources, and/or belonged to groups of people in the lowest classes of society.[11] According to the writers of Matthew (8:20) and Luke (9:58), Jesus admitted that he owned no land or property: "Foxes have holes, and birds of the air have nests; but the Son of Man has nowhere to lay his head." Jesus' disciples left all they had to follow him (Matthew 4:18-22; Mark 1:16-20; Luke 5:1-11; John 1:35-51). Jesus even told the rich young ruler of Matthew 19:16-22 and Luke 18:18-25 to sell all of his possessions and give the money to the poor and follow him. When Jesus gave instructions to seventy disciples preparing to go into the world, he told them to take no possessions with them: "Carry no purse, no bag, no sandals" (Luke 10:4). Jesus' lifestyle and the lifestyle he demanded of his disciples was "characterized by lack of possessions and cutting loose from family ties."[12] Jesus was considered poor by the socioeconomic standards of his day.

Like Dollar, other prosperity gospel preachers assert that Jesus was rich to make their case that God wants all Christians to be rich. In contrast, black prophetic preachers affirm Jesus' poverty to make their case that Jesus identified with and understood the plight of the poor.

Black prophetic preachers have traditionally embraced Jesus' poverty by preaching that his social status enabled him to better identify with the daily lives and struggles of the poor of his day and the poor of our contemporary world. Cheryl Sanders, a professor of ethics at Howard University School of Divinity in Washington, DC, proclaims of Jesus: "He came to us as an unwelcome visitor, as a little baby boy, born in the barn to an unwed mother for whom there was no room in the inn. He came to a poor oppressed people who mistreated him like poor and oppressed people so often mistreat each other, transferring their hostility toward the dominant group to the very one of their own number who would seek to set them free."[13]

In a sermon titled "Can Anything Good Come Out of Nazareth?" Audrey Bronson (founder and pastor of Sanctuary of the Open Door in Philadelphia, Pennsylvania) compared Jesus' childhood neighborhood of Nazareth, which she characterized as a ghetto, to West Philadelphia.[14] Just as the people in the biblical text did not think that anything good could come out of Nazareth because of its lowliness and insignificance, some people feel that nothing good can come out of Philadelphia:

> Jesus is proof that where you come from is not really that important. It is where you are going that matters. There are twenty-five or thirty references in the scriptures that refer to Jesus being from Nazareth. That tells me that you can be in the slums, but the slums do not have to be in you. You see, Nazareth did not make Jesus; instead, Jesus put Nazareth on the map.[15]

Bronson's sermon assured the poor in West Philadelphia that their poverty and life circumstances did not have to define them. To further demonstrate why Jesus was able to identify with the poor, Bronson preached that Jesus entered his world "through the backdoor, on the left side of society" when he was born in an animal stall and wrapped in swaddling clothes.[16] Bronson's African American hearers could identify with the "backdoor" reference since blacks were made to enter the back door of business establishments during the Jim Crow era.[17] Bronson described the "left side" as a place many people feel is "not as good as the right." Her "left side" reference may have resonated with hearers and underscored their economic realities. At the time the sermon was preached, the number of blacks moving into West Philadelphia was increasing along with unemployment and crime while the availability of much-needed public services was decreasing.

Bronson's sermon was also communal. She told the congregation that they could accomplish great things if they worked together. By supporting and encouraging each other, members of the church could benefit as individuals and as a community. While Bronson gave hearers hope that they could rise above their circumstances, she also gave them hope that God was in the process of "resurrecting" West Philadelphia. She ended the sermon by stating "by the power of the ghetto child of Nazareth" good things were coming out of Philadelphia. This sermon was good news to listeners who felt hopeless about their life circumstances.[18]

In some cases, the goals of African American prosperity preachers and African American prophetic preachers are similar. Each recognizes the nihilism or hopelessness that exists in some African American communities and the need to build a sense of self-worth there. Each teaches people that they are of value and worth in the sight of God. Each teaches people that they have salvation through Jesus Christ, that they are fearfully and wonderfully made, that they can do all things through Christ, and that they are beneficiaries of the liberating power of God. Each admonishes people to model their lives after the life of Christ found in the Gospels. The goals of prophetic preachers are reached when their hearers live individual lives that are pleasing to God but become aware of the injustices in the world that impact others and strive to eradicate those injustices. The goals of prosperity preaching are reached when faithful believers live individual lives with which God is pleased and come to embody God's blessings in personal material (financial wealth) and physical (good physical health) ways.

If we examine the quality of the lives of people all over the world, we may be able to agree with the prosperity preachers that poverty is a curse. Not being able to afford some of the necessities of life, such as food, clothing, shelter, and health care, is a curse. Working two or three jobs and still not being able to make a decent living is a curse. Not being able to afford educational opportunities that could qualify working adults for better jobs and thereby improve the quality of their lives is a curse. Not being able to receive treatment for simple ailments that become life threatening when left untreated is a curse. Not being able to access quality primary and secondary education for one's children is a curse. In the Hebrew Bible, a curse was often described as something or someone in opposition to God.[19] Certainly, living a life in which one's basic needs are not met is in opposition to the will of God for all people. However, it is important to distinguish between poverty and the poor.

The World Bank, an organization owned by 187 member countries whose goal is to fight poverty worldwide, helps us to think about poverty even more broadly: "Poverty is pronounced deprivation in well-being, and comprises many dimensions. It includes low incomes and the inability to acquire the basic goods and services necessary for survival with dignity. Poverty also encompasses low levels of health and education, poor access to clean water and sanitation, inadequate physical security, lack of voice, and insufficient capacity and opportunity to better one's life."[20]

This definition highlights the fact that poverty is about more than money. Deprivation of well-being also encompasses the anxieties people experience when they fear for their physical safety or are not valued for who they are. One of the more egregious deprivations is lack of opportunity. People in poverty often are not afforded the chance to change their lives in positive ways. This type of deprivation does not usually happen in isolation. Systems are in place in communities all over the world that perpetuate poverty and doom some people to remain in it. People who are in poverty often do not know how to access programs and services that could help them escape it.

The World Bank's definition also affirms that poverty is a curse. While poverty is a curse, however, the poor are not cursed. The poor are blessed children of God who happen to live in poverty. In Luke 4:18-19 Jesus stood in the synagogue in Nazareth and read from the scroll of the prophet Isaiah, declaring that he came to bring the poor good news. He came to release the captives (who were usually debtors imprisoned by wealthy lenders) and let the oppressed go free. Jesus did not call the poor cursed. Rather, he declared his intent to address the systemic causes of their poverty. As Christians, rather than pointing accusing fingers at the poor because of what they do not have, perhaps we should work together as the body of Christ to embody Jesus' mission to eradicate poverty's systemic causes.

When prosperity preachers talk about poverty, they are not referring only to people who are living below the poverty line. Prosperity preachers define poverty in opposition to wealth. If one is not rich, one is poor. When Leroy Thompson Sr. used the term "rich" in his sermon, he was not referring to those who had all of their basic needs met or those who had a few extra dollars in the bank for emergencies. For Thompson, "That ain't no money!"[21] Prosperity preachers believe that being rich means having money to pay tithes and offerings, while also having money to live lives of luxury as conceptualized in North American capitalistic terms. By defining wealth and poverty in such a binary way, Word of Faith preachers may leave parishioners who are financially comfortable discontent and dissatisfied. Being financially comfortable is not good enough. Having one's needs met is not good enough. Christians must be rich. How much money is enough? At what point should believers be content with what they have? This unending pursuit of material wealth can lead some believers to experience crises of faith if their material wealth does not materialize despite their best efforts.

The poor are not cursed, but poverty is a curse. As people of God, rather than judging and demeaning those who are poor, we should glorify God by sharing of the goods we have and working to eradicate poverty's systemic causes. We all need to be reminded that we do not have to be rich to share what we have with others. We simply need to treat our neighbors the way we would want to be treated if we were to experience financial challenges.

In the next chapter, we will find that prosperity preachers teach their followers that God is the source of not only everything they need but also everything they desire.

NOTES

1. Though Leroy Thompson's congregation is small compared to many other Word of Faith congregations, his books and videos titled *Money Cometh* have been read and viewed by followers all over the world. "Dr. Thompson," Ever Increasing Word Ministries, www.eiwm.org/index.cfm/PageID/1655/index.html (accessed January 22, 2010).

2. Ibid.

3. Creflo Dollar Jr., *Covenant Understanding of Money*, Creflo Dollar Ministries, 2004, compact disc.

4. Creflo Dollar Jr., *Christ in You, the Hope of Glory*, pt. 2, Creflo Dollar Ministries, 2006, compact disc.

5. Kenneth C. Way, "Donkey Domain: Zechariah 9:9 and Lexical Semantics," *Journal of Biblical Literature* 129, no 1 (Spring 2010): 114.

6. Ben Witherington, "The Birth of Jesus," in *The Dictionary of Jesus and the Gospels*, ed. Joel B. Green, Scot McKnight, and I. Howard Marshall (Downer's Grove, IL: InterVarsity, 1992), 69.

7. Kenneth E. Bailey, "The Manger and the Inn: The Cultural Background of Luke 2:7," *The Near East School of Theology Theological Review* 2, no. 2 (1979), 32–36.

8. Ibid., 36–37.

9. Ibid.

10. Some also believe the term "swaddling clothes" to be an indication of Mary and Joseph's social status. René Laurentin writes that swaddling

clothes symbolize the care of the mother while also representing power-lessness and weakness. See René Laurentin, *Les évangiles de l'enfance du Christ* (Paris: Desclee de Brouwer, 1982), 222.

11. P. H. Davids, "Rich and Poor," in *Dictionary of Jesus and the Gospels*, ed. Joel B. Green (Downers Grove, IL: InterVarsity, 1992), 702–3.

12. Colin Brown, "Πτωχος," in *The New International Dictionary of New Testament Theology*, ed. Colin Brown (Exeter, Devon, UK: Paternoster, 1976), 825.

13. Cheryl J. Sanders, "Christ in You, the Hope of Glory," in *Those Preachin' Women*, ed. Ella Pearson Mitchell (Valley Forge, PA: Judson, 1985), 104. Sanders is ordained in the Church of God (Anderson, IN).

14. Audrey Bronson, "Can Anything Good Come Out of Nazareth?" in *Those Preaching Women*, ed. Ella Pearson Mitchell and Jacqueline B. Glass (Valley Forge, PA: Judson, 2004), 80–83.

15. Ibid., 81.

16. Ibid., 82.

17. The Jim Crow era was a period in American history beginning in 1890 in which Southern states instituted laws to segregate the public interactions of blacks and whites. See PBS, *The Rise and Fall of Jim Crow*, Educational Broadcasting Corporation, 2002, www.pbs.org/wnet/jimcrow/stories.html (accessed September 19, 2007).

18. Bronson, "Can Anything Good Come Out of Nazareth?" 83.

19. There are many words in the Hebrew Bible that can be defined as "curse." *Qalal* in the Hebrew Bible means to be despicable, to treat with contempt or dishonor. In Deuteronomy 11:26 when God tells Moses, "See, I am setting before you today a blessing and a curse" (Deuteronomy 11:26), curse is that which is in opposition to God.

20. Jonathan Haughton and Shahidur R. Khandker, *Handbook on Poverty and Inequality* (Washington, DC: World Bank, 2009), 1–2.

21. "Dr. Thompson."

CHAPTER 5

God Is Your Source

Many adherents of the prosperity gospel must have wondered over the years where the money promised by God would come from. Some preachers like Jerry Savelle, founder and CEO of Jerry Savelle Ministries International, of Crowley, Texas,[1] and Leroy Thompson Sr. (whom we studied in chapter 4) prefer to be general in their preaching and just tell their hearers that God is their source. Others tell their adherents particular places (such as the wealth of sinners) through which God chooses to financially bless God's people.

In his weekly podcast in June 2009, Jerry Savelle taught the first of a four-part series titled God Our Source.[2] He began the broadcast by stating his empathy for people who were going through personal financial crises because of the economic downturn. But he wanted to remind everyone that God is the source of everything they need. He cited 2 Corinthians 1:3-4 to establish that God is a God of comfort who has not deserted them. Savelle's series title was inspired by the Amplified Bible version[3] of the passage:

> Blessed be the God and Father of our Lord Jesus Christ, the Father of sympathy (pity and mercy) and the God [Who is the

> Source] of every comfort (consolation and encouragement),
> Who comforts (consoles and encourages) us in every trouble
> (calamity and affliction), so that we may also be able to comfort
> (console and encourage) those who are in any kind of trouble
> or distress, with the comfort (consolation and encouragement)
> with which we ourselves are comforted (consoled and encour-
> aged) by God. (AMP)

Savelle likes the Amplified Version because of its potential
to make people conscious of God's role in their lives. He informed listeners that sometimes other sources dry up, sources
such as banks and lending institutions, friends, and relatives.
They dry up because they were a source rather than *the*
source. God's resources will never dry up.

In his podcast, Savelle also cited Philippians 4:19: "And
my God will liberally supply (fill to the full) your every need
according to His riches in glory in Christ Jesus" (AMP). He
told listeners that the size of the need does not matter. God
can meet it. He shared a bit of his personal journey. Forty
years before he preached that sermon, he had been working
hard to meet the needs of his family. He had also been studying about how to receive from God. That was when he discovered the teaching of seedtime and harvest. He understood
that it is by being obedient to God and sowing seed that God
will meet his needs. Believers do not need to know how God
is going to meet their needs. Their responsibility as people of
faith is simply to believe in God's provision and then expect
to be blessed. God is not only the source of financial blessings
but of guidance, revelation, knowledge, and wisdom. Being
obedient to God's word opens the door to prosperity to anyone who believes.

Savelle also informed his hearers that whenever they do
not have money to sow, they can sow seeds of prayer by praying for others, seeds of service by helping a neighbor in need,
or seeds of encouragement by encouraging someone who was
down.[4] But even though they can sow these other types of

seed, they should not forget that money is a powerful seed. If they do not have money, they should consider selling something and turning that into seed.

In his sermon "Breaking the Generational Curse of Poverty," Leroy Thompson Sr. also taught his people that God is their source. In the sermon, Thompson provided hearers with some basic principles to live by: always keep God first; recognize that God owns everything, you own nothing; God first, others second, you last; God is my source.[5]

Thompson spent most of his time on his fourth point: "God is my source." He said that once Christians truly believe God is the source of everything they need, then God will bless and multiply all the money they sow into the body of Christ. Like Bill Winston (see chapter 3), Thompson taught believers that the money they make on their secular jobs is not intended to support the lifestyle that God wants them to live. Rather, their secular income is seed money, to be sown into ministries so that God can bless them with wealth.

Thompson cited Jeremiah 29:11, explaining that God plans to prosper the people of God by enabling them to have hope for a better future. He also cited 1 Samuel 22:2 as evidence that people who are in debt are distressed and discontent: "Every one that was in distress, and every one that was in debt, and every one that was discontented, gathered themselves unto him; and he became a captain over them: and there were with him about four hundred men" (KJV).

Since God does not want God's people to be distressed and discontent, God has already provided them with everything they need to live prosperous lives. Savelle, Thompson, and other prosperity preachers teach that this divine provision is contained in the promises of God's word. The way prosperity preachers apply the term *promises of God* is very similar to the ways biblical theologians apply it. Biblical theologians study the historical development of doctrine as it appeared chronologically in the Hebrew Bible and New Testament. They believe that there are statements in the Bible that are part of the *promise plan of God*, which is "God's word of declaration, beginning with Eve and continuing on through history, especially in the patriarchs and the Davidic line, that God would continually be in his person and do in his deeds and works (in and through Israel, and later the church) his redemptive plan."[6]

In this way, promises of God are not simply a series of "scattered predictions" unrelated to each other in any way.[7] Rather, the promises of God are part of a divine plan of redemption that starts in Genesis 12:2, where God promised Abraham that God would make of him a great nation, and peaks with the risen Christ. The promise plan of God also includes *threatening aspects or judgments of God* that are consequences if the people of God do not live according to God's will.[8] Prosperity preachers teach their followers that part of God's redemptive plan for humanity is for all people who confess and believe in Jesus Christ to have abundant life, which includes financial wealth and good physical health. As a result, the preachers would argue that all of the individual verses they quote as proof of God's will for Christians to be prosperous are part of God's promise plan, or plan of redemption.

In contrast with Savelle and Thompson, preachers such as Creflo Dollar Jr. offer more specificity about financial sources. In a sermon entitled "Covenant Understanding of Money" preached at World Changers Church International in College Park, Georgia, Dollar taught his listeners about the sources of their financial blessings when they sow seed.[9] Dollar claimed that one source of money for believers was the wealth of sinners. According to Dollar, God caused money to leave the hands of wealthy sinners and make its way into the hands of the righteous. Two of the texts Dollar used to justify these teachings were: "Behold, the hire of the labourers who have reaped down your fields, which is of you kept back by fraud, crieth: and the cries of them which have reaped are entered into the ears of the Lord of sabaoth" (James 5:4, KJV), and "A good man leaveth an inheritance to his children's children:

and the wealth of the sinner is laid up for the just" (Proverbs 13:22, KJV).

James 5:4 is the text to which Dollar is referring in the portion of the sermon highlighted below:

> Now listen, there are two cries right here. The money is crying, but that's not enough. The laborers who labored for the money but don't have it, they are now crying. Now I'm not talking about boohooing. . . . This word is like cry out. It's the same as solicit, publish, confess, or make a demand of. . . . Money is crying. That sounds so strange to me. The wages are crying. Money is tired of being where it was not created to be. Money, which is good, was created to be in the hands of those who are good before God. Money finding its way. Finding its way, "No, I'm not supposed to be here." Finding its way, "No, I'm not supposed to be here." Stock market drop, that was some money that escaped, finding its way. Some rich man lost something, finding its way. Some fat cat lost something else, it's finding its way. . . . We have needed a battle cry all of these years. And the battle cry is, "Money cometh to me now."[10]

Dollar teaches his followers that the money from the defrauded laborers in the ancient world is actually wandering around in the wilderness waiting to be claimed. All believers have to do to claim the money is to cry out by making a demand on the money. He says that the battle cry Christians have needed for a long time to claim the money is Leroy Thompson Sr.'s "Money cometh to me now!" Therefore, believers can claim the money that has been withheld by the wealthy by crying out.

Sifting the Wheat from the Chaff

In relation to James 5:4, almost from the beginning of the book of James, the writer communicates harsh words against the behaviors of *the rich*. In 1:9-10 the writer predicts that

the poor will be raised up or exalted, and the rich will be
made low or humiliated. In 2:6-7 it is the rich who oppress
and drag the members of the assembly into court and blas-
pheme. The problem the writer had with the rich was not that
they had more money than some; it was that they gained their
wealth at the expense of the poor. The writer warned that the
rich would soon endure misery. The money that they were
withholding from the laborers was crying out.[11]

Lord of Sabaoth is a title found in the Hebrew Scriptures
that designated God as both a divine warrior and a divine
king.[12] In this text, believers were made aware that God
saw and knew all. Nothing escaped the knowledge of God.
The use of Lord of Sabaoth here was the author's way of
declaring God to be almighty. "The God who hears the cries
of his suffering people is 'the Lord Almighty,' and he will
vindicate them in due time."[13] God heard the cries of both
the money that had been withheld and the laborers who had
been defrauded. God would make things right. The people in
this text did not have to *cry out* or *make a demand* on their
money to receive the justice of God.

Dollar claimed that Proverbs 13:22 was evidence that the
wealth of the sinner is laid up for the righteous. However,
while the text does affirm Dollar's assertion that the righteous
will inherit the wealth of the sinner, it also raises questions
about to whom this text is referring. Are the *sinners* in the
second part of the verse referring to the "children's children"
who will be left an inheritance by a good man in the first
part of the text? If so, this text may be a warning that sinners
would not receive their rightful *family inheritances* because
of their sin. The inheritance could also be good fortune.[14]
Dollar's teaching that the wealth of sinners was a source of
wealth for the righteous highlights the need for justice. God
sees all that humanity does and rewards those who are faithful and punishes those who are not.

Through his interpretation of both passages, Dollar was
forcing a universal meaning on a text that was composed to

address distinct issues of a particular community. It is quite possible that neither was intended to be a promise of God to all believers for all eternity. Preachers often examine biblical texts and draw parallels to the contemporary world. However, when the preacher contends that particular words of the text are a godly promise, the stakes are raised. When believers understand certain written statements in the Bible to be promises, they not only believe the promises should be fulfilled in their lives, but they also believe they have failed as Christians if promises are not fulfilled. If particular words of a text are not promises, then Christians strive in vain to meet the terms that God has not promised to fulfill.

While prosperity preachers teach their followers that they can have the money that God laid up for the righteous if they would just cry out for it, African American prophetic preachers offer a different perspective. Prophetic preachers may highlight the unjust practices of those who make money on the backs of the poor by underscoring how money secured unjustly is also crying out in our day. In good black prophetic preaching, blame for injustice is not only placed on the rich; it is placed wherever it happens to belong.

For example, if we drive through some inner-city neighborhoods, we may be able to hear the cries of money as we drive by payday lenders and check-cashing establishments that charge exorbitant prices for people to borrow money or even to cash their own checks. We may hear money crying out as we drive by nonprofit agencies that are supposed to be collecting money to provide services for the displaced and poor but use much of the money to line the pockets of select personnel instead. If we listen intently, we may be able to hear cries of money in government buildings where much-needed funds are being wasted, mismanaged, or used to fund programs that are frivolous and unnecessary. If we are not careful, we may hear our own money crying out. We use money that could be used to help people in our communities who are struggling to instead buy an unnecessary pair of shoes, purses, or techno-gadgets so we can look good for a one-time event or impress our friends. In each of these cases, money that is designated for or could benefit the needy is being used by others for their own benefit. God is not pleased.

Earlier in this chapter, I cited a definition of the promise plan of God as a way to understand what prosperity preachers mean when they talk about the promises of God. For biblical theologians and prosperity preachers, the promises of God are not a series of scattered statements that are unrelated to each other. Each statement, both positive and judgmental, is part of God's redemptive plan. One of the major problems with viewing the entire Bible as part of God's redemptive plan that culminates in Jesus Christ is that the distinct messages that God had for the people in a particular time and place in human history get distorted or altogether lost. Even in the cases wherein God made promises to people in the text, did God necessarily intend those promises to apply to all people for all time? Discerning whether a particular phrase in the Bible is intended for all people is not always easy. However, many African American prophetic preachers would simply inform their people that just as God acted on behalf of people in the text, God will also act on their behalf. How God chooses to act is up to God.

Savelle's message was undoubtedly timely for many people who were struggling financially during the 2008 United States economic crisis. His teaching about faith and the need to believe that God could meet their needs was, and is, important for all believers to hear. During his sermon, Savelle emphasized God's ability to meet needs versus God's desire that all believers be rich. Savelle's ability to focus the sermon on what his listeners needed at the time demonstrated his sensitivity to and understanding of their circumstances. However, when he encouraged hearers to sell off items they were not using to get seed, he raised concerns.

In prosperity theology, seed money comes from secular employment. If Savelle's hearers did not have seed money, it may have meant they were unemployed or underemployed. If hearers were in such dire straits that they had to resort to selling items to generate seed, were they also unable to buy food and clothing or pay the rent? If so, should they not use the money generated from selling material goods to meet their immediate needs rather than sow seed? Could having items to sell be a blessing in itself instead of an avenue to larger blessings? In addition, could the need to sell items during tough economic times inspire believers to rethink their consumption during times of plenty? Perhaps instead of buying many items they do not need, they could save and invest some of their money after paying tithes and offerings and making other charitable donations.

One text that prosperity preachers quote often, that could also be helpful when preaching to people who are concerned about their financial futures, is Philippians 4:19, "My God will meet your needs according to the riches of his glory in Christ Jesus." *Chreia* in Greek means necessity or needful thing. In this text, Paul takes time to thank the church of Philippi for their unwavering support of his ministry. Though he maintained his work as a tentmaker, he still needed support from the people of God to fulfill his call as an apostle of Christ. When he wrote, "My God will meet your needs . . . ," he was sharing his personal testimony. He knew from experience that God would supply their needs because God had supplied all of his needs through them, the generous people of the church.

In our individualistic society, we are often told that we need to pull ourselves up by our own bootstraps and make our own way. However, just as God used the people of the church of Philippi to meet Paul's needs, we in the church can come together in difficult and trying times to meet each other's material needs. Many of God's "riches" are contained within the body of Christ in the form of material goods with which we have been blessed. The "riches" of God also include spiritual knowledge and experience that can be used to encourage the downtrodden. When the people of God get together and share out of God's "riches" with one another, many needs can be supplied.

Many prosperity churches regularly provide financial assistance to their members and people in their surrounding communities. However, members who need financial assistance are often looked upon as spiritually weak. After all, if they had enough faith in God, all of their needs would be met. In the Philippians text, Paul reminds the people of God that sometimes we all need help. Sometimes God uses people in our faith communities to provide that help.

Dollar's literal application of James 5:4 through which he advised his hearers to cry out for their money may seem ridiculous to some. However, when people are taught that the Bible literally means what it says, they may not always understand when a text is metaphorical. Though preachers should teach their listeners how to read and interpret texts, listeners should also study the Bible for themselves, ask questions, and find other resources to help them understand the complexities of the Bible.

While there are numerous methodologies for biblical exegesis and responsible interpretation of Scripture, basic steps include (1) reading the text for basic understanding; (2) locating text within immediate context of the chapter and book in which the text is found; (3) defining important and recurring words and phrases; and (4) researching the geography, customs, current events, and politics of people in the text. This particular approach can enable people who read the Bible to mine its depths for deeper understanding.

In this chapter, we found that prosperity preachers teach their followers that God is the source of everything they need. Some of the preachers identify more specific avenues of God's blessings, such as the wealth of sinners, which is laid up for the righteous. Though God is the source of all blessings, as we'll see in chapter 6, many prosperity preachers also teach their listeners that the anointing of God can help them prosper.

NOTES

1. Jerry Savelle has been preaching since 1968. His sermons are broadcast in over two hundred countries. His ministry has offices in Australia, the United Kingdom, and Canada. Savelle is also the founder of Thunder Over Texas, the largest Christian Motorcycle rally in the United States. "About," Jerry Savelle Ministries, www.jerrysavelle.org/ (accessed January 22, 2010).

2. Jerry Savelle, "God Our Source #1," Jerry Savelle Ministries Daily Video Podcast, iTunes, downloaded January 22, 2010.

3. "Amplified Bible Background & History," Lockman Foundation, www.lockman.org/amplified/ (accessed July 7, 2010). The Amplified Bible is a translation first published by Zondervan in 1965 and developed by Frances Siewert in cooperation with the Lockman Foundation. What sets this version apart from others is that it uses synonyms and definitions to explain and expand the meaning of words in the text by placing amplification in parentheses and brackets and after key words or phrases.

4. Jerry Savelle, "God Our Source #2," Jerry Savelle Ministries Daily Video Podcast, iTunes, downloaded July 10, 2010.

5. Leroy Thompson Sr., "Breaking the Generational Curse of Poverty," Ever Increasing Word Ministries, 2005, DVD.

6. Walter Kaiser, *Promise-Plan of God: A Biblical Theology of the Old and New Testaments* (Grand Rapids: Zondervan, 2008), 19.

7. Ibid., 18.

8. Ibid.

9. Creflo Dollar Jr., "Covenant Understanding of Money," Creflo Dollar Ministries, 2004, compact disc.

10. Ibid. The confession "money cometh" was coined by Leroy Thompson Sr. in his book, *Money Cometh! To the Body of Christ* (Tulsa: Harrison House, 1999), 26.

11. Luke Timothy Johnson, *The Letter of James*, Anchor Bible, ed. William Foxwell Albright and David Noel Freedman (New York: Doubleday, 1995), 302.

12. David Noel Freedman, "Lord of Hosts," in *Eerdmans Dictionary of the Bible*, ed. Tony S. L. Michael (Grand Rapids: Eerdmans, 2000), 820–21.

13. Donald W. Burdick, "Hebrews, James, 1, 2 Peter, 1, 2, 3 John, Jude, Revelation," *Expositor's Bible Commentary*, ed. James Montgomery Boice (Grand Rapids: Zondervan, 1981), 200.

14. Raymond Van Leeuwen, *The Book of Proverbs*, New Interpreter's Bible, vol. 5 (Nashville: Abingdon, 1997), 119.

CHAPTER 6

The Anointing Produces Victory

"The true purpose for the anointing is to produce victory in your life so that God may be glorified in the earth." These words were written by Creflo Dollar in a book he wrote very early in his ministry. He defined anointing as "the power to get results in your life."[1] Dollar teaches his followers that when the *super* of the Holy Spirit is smeared or painted on the believer's *natural* self, then the believer becomes *supernatural*. By "supernatural," Dollar means that the believer will be able to accomplish tasks that are beyond her or his natural capabilities to accomplish. Dollar cited 1 John 2 and further defined the *charisma*, usually translated "anointing," as something that is smeared or painted on: "But ye have an unction from the Holy One, and ye know all things" (v. 20, KJV), and "But the anointing which ye have received of him abideth in you, and ye need not that any man teach you: but as the same anointing teacheth you of all things, and is truth, and is no lie, and even as it hath taught you, ye shall abide in him" (v. 27, KJV). Therefore, Dollar believes that the "unction from the Holy One" found in verse 20 is a smearing of the Holy Spirit onto believers that causes them to be supernatural.

The supernatural ability believers receive from the Holy Spirit empowers them for ministry. Christians receive the Holy Spirit upon conversion. After conversion, Christians are able to receive the baptism of the Holy Spirit, which is a deeper dimension of the Spirit that allows them to experience more of the goodness God has in store for God's people. According to Dollar, the Holy Spirit is present in the lives of all believers. Through the Holy Spirit, God gives those called to particular ministries the gifts and abilities to perform those ministries. Dollar also teaches that any teacher of the Bible can teach and any preacher can preach. However, when the teacher or preacher is anointed by God for the office of teaching and preaching, he or she can then teach and preach with power that is lacking in those without those particular anointings.[2] While some preachers teach that the anointing in the lives of people who are called to certain offices is different from the ordinary anointing that operates in the lives all believers,[3] Dollar believes that the degree of anointing operating in the lives of believers can be increased by fasting and prayer.[4]

However, in addition to believing that the anointing empowers people for ministry, Dollar also believes that the anointing facilitates material prosperity. In a sermon titled "Levels of the Anointing," Dollar used several Scriptures to support his contention that the anointing gives believers power not only to do the work of God, but also to have "stuff," or material goods, restored to them that Satan took away. "I'm telling you, God will not forget everything that's been stolen and affected. He's about to cause restoration to hit your house. I don't think you understand what I'm saying. I've got some stuff that's going to be restored back to me that that devil never had any business putting his hands on, and it's coming back."[5]

Dollar teaches his followers that restoration is one of the outcomes of the anointing. When believers have lost dignity, strength, family, friends, hope, or even the will to live, the anointing can cause them to receive supernatural restoration.[6]

As proof that God will restore material goods that Satan took away, Dollar cited Joel 2:23-26:

> Be glad then, ye children of Zion, and rejoice in the LORD your God: for he hath given you the former rain moderately, and he will cause to come down for you the rain, the former rain, and the latter rain in the first month. And the floors shall be full of wheat, and the vats shall overflow with wine and oil. And I will restore to you the years that the locust hath eaten, the cankerworm, and the caterpillar, and the palmerworm, my great army which I sent among you. And ye shall eat in plenty, and be satisfied, and praise the name of the LORD your God, that hath dealt wondrously with you: and my people shall never be ashamed. (KJV)

For Dollar, rain in the text symbolizes the anointing. The coming of the Holy Spirit at Pentecost is a manifestation of the latter rain, or latter anointing. Former rain, or former anointing, is the Holy Spirit as experienced by the prophets of the Hebrew Bible.[7] According to Dollar, this Scripture promises believers that God will cause both the anointing of the prophets and the anointing of Pentecost to fall at the same time. Such a tremendous outpouring of the anointing will be a great blessing to all believers. When the great anointing occurs, God will restore to believers material goods that have been stolen from them by Satan over the years, and believers will live in plenty.

Dollar's teaching about the latter and former rain is consistent with the teaching of the Latter Rain movement in the Pentecostal church, which began in 1947. The Latter Rain movement was characterized by healing and other "miraculous phenomena."[8] It also stressed the imminent (possibly any day) return of Jesus, which would be preceded by an outpouring of the Holy Spirit in accordance with the "former rain" and the "latter rain" of Joel 2:23. Joel 2:23 was interpreted in the movement as a dual prophecy of the day of Pentecost of

Acts 2 and the outpouring of the Holy Spirit that will precede Jesus' second coming. The Latter Rain movement was gaining popularity at the time when preachers such as Oral Roberts and Billy Graham were also gaining popularity.

Sifting the Wheat from the Chaff

Dollar's literal interpretation offers one perspective of the text. Some contemporary biblical exegetes offer other alternatives. The book of Joel was written as the prophet's response to an invasion of locusts in Jerusalem.[9] The invasion of locusts was so pervasive and life-altering that the prophet felt the insects were agents of God sent to bring judgment on a disobedient nation. The major theme of Joel was the Day of Yahweh, which was an appointed time during which God would act. Joel presented two alternatives for God's action: salvation and destruction. In 1:1–2:17, Joel wrote of the destruction of Israel, in which Yahweh led an army of nations to destroy Israel.[10] In 2:18–4:17, the prophet wrote of the salvation of Israel, in which Yahweh delivered Israel from annihilation and destroyed nations that were seeking Israel's demise.[11]

According to some scholars, in the Old Testament, the early rain was an autumn rain that usually fell between late October and early December. The autumn rain usually broke the summer drought.[12] The latter rain usually fell in the spring between March and April. This latter rain helped to facilitate good harvest by preventing grain from drying up in the fields.[13] When the prophet wrote that the rain was going to fall as before, he meant that the whole cycle of rain (which included both the autumn and spring rains), would fall in accordance with their former regularity and levels.[14] Yahweh promised restitution for the damages caused by the locust invasions. In this interpretation, rain was not representative of the Holy Spirit. Joel informed the community about the outpouring of the Holy Spirit in verses 28-29, which would occur after the physical rain had fallen. Therefore, rain in verse 23 was literally water from God to restore the crops that had suffered loss. However, even taking a metaphorical interpretation of the text, the ultimate message is that God's blessings (in the form of rain in an agricultural economy) comes in cycles. The promise is that no matter how bad the current season is, the next season will ultimately follow.

During the economic recession, Dollar preached many sermons designed to encourage his hearers. In a sermon titled "The Right Attitude about the Recession," Dollar advised his hearers to change their thinking about the recession in particular and the relationship between God and the world in general. In this sermon, Dollar reminded listeners that the power of the anointing enabled believers to have all of their needs met even in times of economic crisis:

> The financial crisis that is going on in the world today—that's the world's crisis. It is not the church's crisis. It's not the body of Christ's crisis. We are not participating in the recession because we are operating by the kingdom of God and we trust God to take care of us. And we are not going to fear. Money is the world's power. But agape love is the power of the Christian. The anointing is the power of the Christian. And when you are operating in that agape love and operating in the anointing, then all of your needs are going to be met by the supply that God has in heaven. And you are going to have to trust God.[15]

BLACK PROPHETIC PREACHING AND THE ANOINTING

In a sermon titled "Spiritual Empowerment: A Closer Look," Classy Preston, pastor of Pleasant Grove Church of Cary, North Carolina, approached the ability of the Holy Spirit to empower believers in a very different way than Dollar. She highlighted the ability of the Holy Spirit to empower women to combat sexism.[16] After observing the ways she witnessed the Holy Spirit working in the lives of her mother and grandmother as a child, Preston pointed out the dilemma of many gifted African American women who are capable and clearly gifted by the Spirit to do wonderful work in their churches but are hindered by a culture of gender discrimination. Preston used Mary Magdalene as an example of a woman who was written off by society because of her demon possession. However, through the work of the Holy Spirit, she was empowered to spread the gospel. Mary Magdalene had been "powerless to overcome" the demonic forces within her before she met Jesus. Jesus changed the course of her life. Whereas she had been defeated and anxious, she became victorious and self-assured.

The new Mary Magdalene was the first disciple at the tomb on Easter morning. The new Mary Magdalene was the one who informed Peter and John that Jesus was not in the tomb. The new Mary Magdalene was the one who was the first to see and speak to Jesus. The new Mary Magdalene was the first to spread the core gospel, "I have seen the Lord! He is risen indeed." This new Mary Magdalene was bold and empowered because of her encounter with Jesus and the presence of the Holy Spirit in her life. Mary Magdalene's role in the early church was vital and essential to the spreading of the gospel in the same ways the role of women in the church and world is vital two thousand years later.

Preston ended her sermon with a hopeful prophetic declaration: "The world needs sensitive and spiritually empowered women today. It might be that without them, our civilization will falter and die. But with the wisdom and courage with which Jesus empowers the once suppressed female half of the world's population, our brightest days may yet be just ahead."[17] For Preston, the Holy Spirit is at work in the lives of women who are empowered to do God's work in the world. The cultures of the world need to change by acknowledging, accepting, and making room for the empowered women to work.

As mentioned above, Dollar cites 1 John 2:20 and 27 as evidence that the anointing imbues believers with power, not just for ministry, but to aid them in every aspect of their lives. The term *charisma*, translated "unction" or "anointing," literally means anything that is smeared on, such as ointment or oil. In the Old Testament, priests, prophets, and kings were anointed when they were appointed by God to a particular call. For example, Aaron and his sons were anointed with oil by Moses in Leviticus 8:1-13. In the text, the anointing was done to sanctify, set apart, dedicate, or consecrate them. In 1 Samuel 10:1, Saul was anointed with oil by Samuel when God appointed him king over Israel. In the text, Saul was anointed to be a leader, ruler, captain, or prince over God's territory or possession. In 2 Samuel 5:3, David was anointed king over Israel. In each of these cases, the persons were anointed or smeared with oil in order to assume tasks to which God had called them. In none of these texts do we find that the anointing actually bestowed power. However, implicit in the text is the understanding that the anointing was a sign of God's calling and power at work in the lives of the people whom God had called. The Day of Pentecost was when God conferred disciples of Christ with power for ministry: "But ye shall receive power, after that the Holy Ghost is come upon you: and ye shall be witnesses unto me both in Jerusalem, and in all Judaea, and in Samaria, and unto the uttermost part of the earth" (Acts 1:8, KJV).

After the Spirit came on Pentecost, Peter, who had betrayed Jesus, was emboldened by the Spirit to preach to the crowd that had gathered in Jerusalem. Three thousand people were added to the church that day. The anointing as power for ministry is certainly biblically founded and taught in many different Christian denominations. However, the anointing as a means to financial prosperity is not founded in the biblical text. In the latter part of the nineteenth century, teachers of the Higher Life or Keswick movement taught their followers that the main purpose of the Holy Spirit is to empower believers to serve the church. Dollar differs from these teachers in his belief that the anointing helps believers acquire material goods.

Dollar's characterization of Joel 2:23 as a prophecy for restoration of material goods to Christians in the twenty-first century ignores the message that the prophet was communicating to the community of Israel. The prophet Joel was predicting the time when God would send physical rain to end the existing drought. Joel's prophecy gave hope to a people who wondered whether God had indeed forsaken or forgotten them. Dollar's interpretation of the text allegorized rain (turned it into a symbol) for the anointing. By insisting that the prophet was referring to material goods, or "stuff," when he used the term *restore*, Dollar interpreted the text in light of a twenty-first-century, North American, capitalistic context.

While Dollar focused primarily on empowerment to become rich, Classy Preston emphasized the way the Holy Spirit empowered and emboldened Mary Magdalene to become a disciple. Before she met Jesus, Mary Magdalene was marginalized by society. After meeting Jesus, she became a bold leader who was not afraid to share the gospel. Preston preached that women have gifts that God gives them to share. The world needs to embrace them so everyone can be blessed by them.

The anointing gives believers power to fulfill their calls in ministry. However, according to prosperity preachers, as we'll see in chapter 7, believers also need to claim their authority in Christ in order to live the most prosperous Christian lives they possibly can.

NOTES

1. Creflo Dollar Jr., *Understanding God's Purpose for the Anointing* (Edmond, OK: Vision Communications, 1992), 14.

2. Kenneth E. Hagin, *Understanding the Anointing* (Tulsa: Kenneth Hagin Ministries, 1983), 41. Dollar adopts much of his understanding of the anointing from Kenneth Hagin.

3. Ibid., 37.

4. Dollar, *Understanding God's Purpose for the Anointing*, 56–64.

5. "Levels of the Anointing, Part I," Creflo Dollar Ministries, www.creflodollarministries.org/Broadcast/Broadcast.aspx (accessed January 10, 2006).

6. Ibid.

7. Dollar, *Understanding God's Purpose for the Anointing*.

8. Richard Riss, "The Latter Rain Movement of 1948," *Journal of the Society for Pentecostal Studies* 4, no. 1 (1982): 35.

9. David Allan Hubbard, *Joel and Amos*, Tyndale Old Testament Commentaries (Downers Grove, IL: InterVarsity, 1989), 21.

10. Ibid.

11. Ibid.

12. Ibid., 65–66.

13. Ibid.

14. Ibid.

15. Creflo Dollar, "The Right Attitude in Recession," Creflo Dollar Ministries, iTunes, downloaded January 10, 2010.

16. Classy Preston, "Spiritual Empowerment: A Closer Look," in *Those Preaching Women: African American Preachers Tackle Tough Questions*, ed. Ella Pearson Mitchell (Valley Forge, PA: Judson, 1996), 85–92.

17. Ibid., 92.

CHAPTER 7

There Is Authority in the Name of Jesus

"But you've got to know that when you speak that name, something's about to happen."[1] With this statement, founder and pastor of the Living Word Christian Center in Oak Park, Illinois, Bill Winston was reminding his followers that there is authority in the name of Jesus. When believers verbally confess their belief in Jesus' authority, they can experience miraculous breakthroughs in every aspect of their lives.

According to Winston, believers can only realize their spiritual potential when they understand the power that is at their disposal. When they accept Jesus as their Lord and Savior, they are also granted access to the authority of the name of Jesus. Whatever they need or desire can come to pass if they call on the name of Jesus on their own behalf. Winston cited Matthew 28:16-18 as evidence of the authority given to all who believe:

> Then the eleven disciples went away into Galilee, into a moun-
> tain where Jesus had appointed them. And when they saw him,
> they worshipped him: but some doubted. And Jesus came and
> spake unto them, saying, All power is given unto me in heaven

and in earth. Go ye therefore, and teach all nations, baptizing them in the name of the Father, and of the Son, and of the Holy Ghost: Teaching them to observe all things whatsoever I have commanded you: and, lo, I am with you always, even unto the end of the world. Amen. (KJV)

Winston taught his listeners that since Jesus was given all power, then Christians have the same power that Jesus has if they believe. He stated that the name of Jesus is a substitute for Jesus himself. Jesus is alive, and though he is no longer on earth with us, he is doing the same work he did while he was here. He simply does the work of God through his name. Believers have access to Jesus and to his power through his name.

This teaching is not new. In his sermon "Our Words Dominate Our Lives," Kenneth Hagin taught his followers to access the authority of Christ through positive confession. Hagin took the title of the sermon directly from one of E. W. Kenyon's writings: "Our words snare us and hold us in captivity or they set us free and become powerful in the lives of others. It is what we confess with our lips that really dominates our inner being. When we realize that we will never rise above our confession, we are getting to the place where God can really begin to use us."[2]

According to this theology, Christians will either rise or fall to the level of their confessions of faith. In the sermon, Hagin told several stories to make his point: the story about how he himself confessed for a down payment on a house and subsequently received it; the story of how his wife confessed for new draperies for the new house and then received them; and the story of Caleb and Joshua in Numbers 13:30 confessing that they were able to conquer the land and doing just that.

In another sermon titled "We Have Been Authorized by Jesus," Hagin combined theology with personal and biblical stories to help his hearers understand his point. He taught that believers have access to all of the authority that Christ was given on earth and in heaven.³ Having access to Christ's authority means believers have the right to be healed, to be made righteous, to be sanctified, to be wise, or to be redeemed.⁴ To receive those rights from God, all believers need only claim them.

In his sermon, Hagin told his hearers about a vision God gave him. In the vision, Jesus was standing in front of a kneeling Hagin. While Jesus was talking, a demon jumped in front of him saying, "Yakety, yak, yak. Yakety, yak, yak," and placed a screen of smoke in between Jesus and Hagin. Unable to hear what Jesus was saying, Hagin wondered why the Lord was allowing this to happen. Without thinking about it, Hagin spoke to the spirit and said, "I command you, in the name of the Lord Jesus Christ, to shut up and to stop!" The demon hit the floor, and the screen of smoke disappeared. Jesus then told Hagin, "If you hadn't done something about that, I couldn't have." In the dream, Hagin was stunned by Jesus' words.

Hagin explained in the sermon what Jesus meant: There is no place in the New Testament where any writer told the church to pray to God the Father about the devil or to pray to God the Father to rebuke the devil. "People who ask God to rebuke the devil are wasting their time. You see, the least member in the Body of Christ has just as much authority over the devil as anyone else. Unless believers do something about the devil, nothing will be done."⁵

Since the theology Hagin used for his sermon originated with Kenyon, we will examine Kenyon's use of Scripture to better understand the Word of Faith teachings about authority and positive confession.

Faith and Positive Confession

Kenyon used Hebrews 4:14-16 as evidence that believers should confess in order to receive from God. "Seeing then that we have a great high priest, that is passed into the heavens,

Jesus the Son of God, let us hold fast our profession. For we have not an high priest which cannot be touched with the feeling of our infirmities; but was in all points tempted like as we are, yet without sin. Let us therefore come boldly unto the throne of grace, that we may obtain mercy, and find grace to help in time of need" (KJV). For Kenyon, the authority of Jesus and positive confession were interrelated. God granted Jesus authority, and believers have access to Jesus' authority through positive confession. In this text, Kenyon considered the word *profession* to have the same meaning as *confession*.

Sifting the Wheat from the Chaff

Like all biblical texts, this text is packed with meaning that could yield multiple interpretations. When reading the letter to the Hebrews, it is apparent that the writer was attempting to encourage people who were losing their faith. They were tired of worship, tired of being viewed as different in their society, and tired of trying to pray.[6] Some were even considering leaving the community. The writer wanted to assure hearers that human affairs, which seemed random and chaotic, were instead being overseen and presided over by the divine Son who was seated at the right hand of God and "sustains all things by his powerful word." One of the purposes of Hebrews 4 was to encourage the congregation to engage in "daring" and even "audacious prayer" by approaching the throne of God with boldness.[7]

For the author of this text, the nature of prayer, whether bold or timid, was dependent on what the community members believed about God and God's relationship to them.[8] Therefore, if the members believed that Jesus was the Son of God as they professed and that God would hear and answer their prayers, they needed to pray boldly. That was why the writer was encouraging the community to hold fast to their "profession" that Jesus is the Son of God and "the reflection of God's glory and the exact imprint of God's very being" (Hebrews 1:3).[9]

Kenyon cited John 16:23-24 as further evidence of the authority that believers had when they employed the name of Jesus: "And in that day ye shall ask me nothing. Verily, verily, I say unto you, Whatsoever ye shall ask the Father in my name, he will give it you. Hitherto have ye asked nothing in my name: ask, and ye shall receive, that your joy may be full" (KJV).

One biblical scholar has suggested that the language used in John 16:23 signaled a change in the relationship between Jesus and his disciples.[10] In the Greek, the first "ask" of verse 23 was a translation of the verb *erotao*, which could mean both "to make a petition" and "to ask a question."[11] The second "ask," *aiteo*, usually meant "to make a petition."[12] The writer may have intended for both types of asking to be represented.

Since the disciples would no longer be able to approach Jesus physically to ask him questions, they needed to learn to whom to direct their questions. They also needed to understand how to make petitions. As a result, the first change in the disciples' relationship to Jesus was that their questions would be answered with the help of the Holy Spirit. The second change in their relationship with Jesus would be their ability to share in Jesus' work as his *friends*. Thus, the petitions referred to in this text were not random petitions about anything they desired. Rather, the petitions they made to God were to be related to the work of God they were called to do in the world. As such, their petitions would be based on their desire to love and obey God.

One of the tremendous gifts that the prosperity gospel makes to its followers is the belief that through Christ they can do all things. Though this message is one disseminated in many Christian denominations thanks to the apostle Paul's letter to the church at Philippi (Philippians 4:13), prosperity theology's teaching about the authority of Christ challenges Christians not to limit their thinking to the confines of their day-to-day realities. Christians are only limited by their abilities to believe in the omnipotence of God and to confess their authority to access God's power through the name of Jesus. They should think big and dream big because they serve a big God. For this reason, some people find prosperity theology liberating. Christians can defy the limitations that society tries to impose on them by appealing not to just *a* higher power but to *the highest power*.

While some people find prosperity preaching liberating, there are others who find it debilitating. One young woman who is a former member of a prosperity church recalled the time when she test-drove cars she could not afford and then told salespeople that Jesus was going to take care of her payments. She was taught that she could use her authority in Jesus Christ by confessing anything in Jesus' name and receive it. She never received the car she sought.[13] She was also taught that if her claims did not become a reality, she was at fault—she must not have done something right. She felt disillusioned and stupid for having ever believed God would grant her request. While prosperity preaching can build self-confidence, it can also cause adherents to have crises of faith.

In the Great Commission of Matthew 28:16-20, Jesus said that he had been given all power in heaven and earth. In this text, Jesus charged the disciples to go baptize and make disciples of all nations. They also were to teach those nations what Jesus had taught them. The mission that Jesus was calling the disciples to accomplish was rooted in the authority of Jesus. There is authority in Jesus' name. However, the authority of Jesus' name is to be used to do the work of Jesus Christ. In the Great Commission, Jesus told the disciples that all authority in heaven and on earth had been given to him. God imbued Jesus with all authority. With that authority, Jesus commissioned the disciples to baptize and to teach the people to obey the words he had taught them. The authority of the name of Jesus was not given, as Kenneth Hagin taught, to pursue personal material gain. The authority in the name of Jesus was to be used by the disciples to disseminate the good news.

The Hebrews 4:14-16 text did not instruct believers to make positive confessions about their general needs and desires. Nor did this text support Kenyon's contention that believers did not need to ask to be healed, to be made righteous, to be sanctified, to be wise, or to be redeemed. The writer of the text did confirm that God would hear and respond to the petitions of believers when they prayed.

From an African American prophetic preacher's perspective, this text is very good news. This text can empower those who may feel powerless. For example, though African American women have made major strides in attaining equality in many aspects of our society, many still have a long way to go. Some are still subjected to verbal and emotional abuse at the hands of partners who are supposed to love them. Some are told that they are worthless. Some are told that they are not smart enough to get into college or work in particular fields, so they should not even try. Some are told they are incompetent. Some are told that they will never amount to anything.

With this text, the sisters can take heart. They do not have to be content with how other people see them. They can reach higher and discern God's vision. They can ask God what God's will is for their lives. God will answer their questions. And through the power of the Holy Spirit, God will guide them into being the people God is calling them to be. Through the power of the Holy Spirit, they can overcome the negative images by embracing new self-images—images based on God's view rather than human views. No one can tell them what they cannot do, because God has a purpose and plan for them.

Prosperity preachers teach their followers that through the name of Jesus Christ, they have authority to do all things.

One of the acts believers are able to do using Christ's authority is to claim their physical healing.

NOTES

1. Bill Winston, "Faith in the Name of Jesus," Bill Winston Ministries, http://bwmbroadcast.org/player/flash?stream=BW630.mp4 (accessed May 15, 2010).

2. E. W. Kenyon and Don Gossett Kenyon, *The Power of Your Words* (New Kensington, PA: Whitaker House, 1977), 27–28.

3. E. W. Kenyon, *Jesus the Healer* (Lynnwood, WA: Kenyon's Gospel Publishing Society, 1940), 59.

4. Ibid., 17–18.

5. Kenneth E. Hagin, "We Have Been Authorized by Jesus," *Word of Faith*, September 1999, 5–7.

6. Thomas G. Long, *Hebrews*, Interpretation Bible Commentary (Louisville: Westminster John Knox, 1997), 3.

7. Ibid.

8. Ibid., 64. Long further writes that theological confession about Jesus emboldens prayer by addressing the issue of approachability of God. Believers need to believe that they have every right to approach God. However, he also writes that "true prayer is prefaced by awe" and a sense of human unworthiness. Long believes that the Christian faith teaches us that no one is worthy to pray except Jesus who is without sin (Hebrews 4:15). However, God's work in Jesus makes our prayer possible.

9. Ibid.

10. Rodney A. Whitacre, *John* (Downers Grove, IL: InterVarsity, 1999), 396.

11. *Erotao* can mean to put a query to someone or to ask a question or to ask for something or to make a request. In addition, *erotao* can also refer to making a request of someone on someone else's behalf. F. W. Danker and W. Bauer, *A Greek-English Lexicon of the New Testament and Other Early Christian Literature* (Chicago, IL: University of Chicago Press, 2000), 395.

12. *Aiteo* is defined as making a request of someone for an answer or to demand. See Danker and Bauer, *A Greek-English Lexicon*, 30.

13. "The Prosperity Gospel—When Paying Tithes Goes Wrong," The Tithing Hoax, http://thetithinghoax.com/the-prosperity-gospel-when-paying-tithes-goes-wrong/ (accessed October 1, 2011).

CHAPTER 8

Claim Your Healing

"Claim your healing" was Bill Winston's advice to his listeners in a sermon titled "Jesus Healed Them All."[1] Winston started his sermon by telling his congregation that while God wants everyone to be healthy, some people try to insert doubt into Scriptures where there is no doubt. He then began to recount narratives in the Bible in which the characters had good relationships with God until they began to doubt. Satan put doubt in Eve's mind. Peter began to sink when he began to doubt. Job had a good relationship with God until Satan interfered. Winston cited Job 3:25-26 to show that fear and worry caused Job to lose faith: "For the thing which I greatly feared is come upon me, and that which I was afraid of is come unto me. I was not in safety, neither had I rest, neither was I quiet; yet trouble came" (KJV).

Winston wanted to convince his hearers that doubt is the enemy of faith. According to his understanding, believers need to have faith in God to be healed. To help his hearers develop faith in the ability and willingness of God to heal, Winston told the story of Jesus healing in a crowd in Luke 4:40. Jesus had just healed Simon's mother-in-law who had been sick with a fever. When he rebuked her fever, she rose and started serving those who had gathered in Simon's house. But word spread and people brought Jesus crowds of people who had many different diseases. And Jesus healed every one of them.

Jesus did not heal *some* of the crowd, Winston emphasized. No, not one person left that encounter sick. Jesus healed them all. In doing so, Jesus was walking in the will of God. In fact, healing was part of the salvation that Jesus ultimately accomplished on Calvary. Salvation and healing were both achieved on the cross. Just as Jesus healed all the people in the crowd, God had already healed everyone listening to Winston's sermon. "Healing belongs to you," Winston told his hearers. God had healed them two thousand years ago.

Though Winston did not quote the text directly in this sermon, when he and other prosperity preachers assert that salvation and healing were taken care of on Calvary, they are alluding to Isaiah 53:4-5, from one of the Servant Songs: "Surely he hath borne our griefs, and carried our sorrows: yet we did esteem him stricken, smitten of God, and afflicted. For he was wounded for our transgressions, he was bruised for our iniquities: the chastisement of our peace was upon him; and with his stripes we are healed" (KJV). Word of Faith theology, as well as the theologies of many Protestant denominations, teaches followers that the suffering servant of Isaiah 53 is Jesus Christ. Therefore, this text testifies not only to the suffering that Jesus endured to bear human sin, but physical sickness and disease as well.

The Law of Positive Confession

Prosperity preachers believe in the law of positive confession, which has two aspects. First, believers must confess that they have something (e.g., healing, material goods) *before* it is manifested in their lives.[2] When believers make their confession, "By his stripes I am healed," they must believe that they *are* healed before the symptoms leave their bodies.[3]

The second aspect of positive confession is that, since believers will never rise above their confessions, they should never make a negative confession. For example, they should never say they have cancer or pneumonia after receiving the diagnosis from a doctor. By talking about their diseases, they are glorifying Satan, who has the ability to inflict them with disease. Because God has redeemed believers from Satan's reign, it is imperative for Christians to confess that Satan has no right to reign over them with sickness, disease, weakness, or failure.[4] When Christians make positive confessions, even after receiving negative diagnoses, they are embracing God's promise for health and wholeness and rejecting Satan's right to affect their lives.

Prosperity preachers teach their followers that sickness and disease do not belong in the body of Christ. In fact, according to prosperity theology, sickness among the people of God is evidence of lack of knowledge, lack of faith,[5] or broken fellowship with God.[6] Many Word of Faith preachers believe, as E. W. Kenyon also taught, that it is abnormal for Christians to go to physicians for healing.[7] There are no cases of sickness and disease that God does not want to heal. Indeed, it is not the will of God for anyone to die of disease.[8]

Today's Word of Faith preachers have adopted Kenyon's teaching, which connects sin to sickness and disease. Just as Jesus' resurrection settled the problems of sickness and disease, it also settled the problem of sin. There is no sin problem.[9] Sin has been handled. Sin and sickness come from the same source—Satan. Therefore, just as Jesus' resurrection took care of the problems of sickness and disease, it also took care of the condemnation of sin. When a person is born again, all sins are forgiven and the sin nature is replaced by the nature of God. Moreover, disease is eradicated along with the forgiven sin.[10]

Sifting the Wheat from the Chaff

In the Luke 4:40 text, Jesus did indeed heal all of the people. This text serves as evidence of the healing power of God at work in Jesus Christ in the text and also in the lives of those of us who have decided to follow Christ. When Winston teaches his followers that Jesus healed all of the people, he employs "all" to mean the total number of people in Jesus' presence at the time. However, Winston misses the opportunity to highlight other senses of the word "all," for example, that Jesus healed "all" of the people in a sense of restoration of wholeness.

All of the people Jesus healed were able to assume their former places in their communities. When Jesus healed Simon's mother, she immediately got up and started serving. When Jesus healed the woman with the issue of blood in Mark 5:21-34, he called her "daughter." Her blood disease had made her an outcast of her community. After her healing, she could return to her community and resume her role in it, whatever that may have been. In other cases, Jesus' healing enabled people to be spiritually restored to right relationship with God. In these cases, when Jesus healed, he also forgave sins. For example, in Matthew 9:2 Jesus healed a man who was paralyzed. Jesus told the man that his sins were forgiven. The man was immediately able to rise, pick up the bed on which he had been brought to Jesus, and walk. In this case, healing and forgiveness of sins were related. But are healing and sin always related?

Sin and Disease in the Bible

In the Old Testament, sin and disease are *sometimes* related. There are occasions when Scripture indicates that Yahweh punished disobedience by inflicting the people with diseases. In the Exodus narrative, God subjected the people of Egypt to ten plagues after Moses appealed to Pharaoh to allow the

Israelites to be released from the bondage of slavery and leave Egypt. After initially agreeing to Moses' request, Pharaoh's heart was hardened by God, and he refused to let the people go. One of the subsequent plagues was boils on humans and animals: "And the LORD said unto Moses and unto Aaron, Take to you handfuls of ashes of the furnace, and let Moses sprinkle it toward the heaven in the sight of Pharaoh. And it shall become small dust in all the land of Egypt, and shall be a boil breaking forth with blains [blisters, boils] upon man, and upon beast, throughout all the land of Egypt" (Exodus 9:8-9, KJV).

In Deuteronomy 28:22, sickness was not only used as punishment but was characterized as a curse. The Israelites were told that among the curses that God would impose upon those who were disobedient was sickness: "The LORD shall smite thee with a consumption [wasting disease], and with a fever, and with an inflammation, and with an extreme burning [violent fever], and with the sword, and with blasting, and with mildew; and they shall pursue thee until thou perish" (KJV).

In Leviticus, among the many laws the Israelites needed to follow to please God are found blessings for good behavior and penalties for bad behavior. For example, Leviticus 26:15-16 declares: "And if ye shall despise my statutes, or if your soul abhor my judgments, so that ye will not do all my commandments, but that ye break my covenant: I also will do this unto you; I will even appoint over you terror, consumption, and the burning ague, that shall consume the eyes, and cause sorrow of heart: and ye shall sow your seed in vain, for your enemies shall eat it" (KJV).

However, sickness was not caused by disobedience in the case of King Hezekiah, who was "sick unto death" (Isaiah 38:1). When the prophet Isaiah visited the king to warn him of impending death, Hezekiah went to God with a prayerful plea that the Lord would remember his righteous life: "Then Hezekiah turned his face toward the wall, and prayed unto the LORD, and said, Remember now, O LORD, I beseech thee, how I have walked before thee in truth and with a perfect heart, and have done that which is good in thy sight. And Hezekiah wept sore" (vv. 2-3, KJV). No explanation is given in the text for Hezekiah's sickness. However, after the king reminded God of how faithful he, Hezekiah, had been, the Lord added fifteen years to his life.

The Israelite worldview of illness as punishment for sin is also present in the New Testament.[11] Using some New Testament texts, one could make the argument that sin and disease are connected in such a way that when sin is forgiven, disease is cured. After all, Jesus did, in certain texts, heal by forgiving sin. For example, in Mark 2:5 Jesus healed a paralytic who was brought to him and lowered through the roof of a home in Capernaum by four of his friends by saying, "Son, thy sins be forgiven thee" (KJV). Jesus again connected sin and disease when, after healing the paralytic at the pool of Bethesda, he said, "Do not sin any more, so that nothing worse happens to you" (John 5:14).

However, this argument could easily be refuted by John 9:3. Here Jesus responded to one of the disciples who asked whether the blind man or his parents sinned in order for the man to have been born blind by saying, "Neither hath this man sinned, nor his parents; but that the works of God should be made manifest in him" (KJV). In healing texts such as the woman with the blood disease in Luke 8:43-48, Jesus healed according to the faith of the one being healed. Sin is not mentioned in the text.

We see that in the Old Testament and the New Testament, disease was not always punishment for sin and healing was not always a consequence of forgiveness of sin. The text at the center of prosperity theology's doctrine of healing is Isaiah 53:4-5. Many biblical scholars agree that Isaiah 40–50 was written during the time of Babylonian exile while large populations of the Jewish community were living as captives in a strange land (between 550 and 515 BCE). While in

Babylon, the exiles from Judah lived along the banks of the Euphrates and were surrounded by worshippers of Marduk and Nebo and other Babylonian gods. During this period, the exiles tried to understand how they as people of God had come to be a scattered and discarded people. The exile was a time of spiritual searching in which priests, prophets, and laity sought answers to their spiritual questions.[12]

The spiritual history of the people of Judah and Israel was fraught with disobedience of a people with whom God had established a covenant relationship. God had given the community commandments by which to live their lives. Yet over and over again, the people had failed to walk according to God's statutes. They had worshipped other gods and lived according to their own wills. As a solution to this ongoing problem of sin and punishment, God called on the services of the servant.

Scholars differ on the identity of the servant. Some believe him to have been Jeremiah or a Jeremiah-type figure who was chosen by God to be a prophet among the people of Israel and Judah.[13] As a prophet, the servant's job was to constantly remind the people that they needed to repent of their sins and turn back to God. The message of repentance was met with opposition and resistance. The servant was deemed a "suffering servant" because he was ridiculed, ostracized, and threatened with death or bodily harm because of his message.

Consistent with the teachings of E. W. Kenyon, many Word of Faith preachers teach their followers that the suffering servant of Isaiah was Jesus and that Jesus literally bore all human sickness and disease. In church history, there is a long tradition of interpreting this passage Christologically. However, when Christ is read into the text, the original messages for the people of Israel get lost. As people of God, the Israelites were supposed to obey God and follow God's commandments. However, time and time again, the Israelites sinned and were punished by God for their transgressions. The servant of Isaiah was God's solution to Israel's sin and punishment problem. However, the work of reconciliation, trying to get the people of Israel to repent of their evil ways and turn back to God, is negated when Christ is interpreted as the servant.

By interpreting Isaiah 53 out of context, Kenyon did not consider that sickness may have been used as a metaphor in 53:4 for the distress present in Israel as a result of sin. As a result, to claim that Christians should use this particular text as evidence of the healing they are able to receive through the suffering of Jesus Christ does not honor the context.

One widely held belief in prosperity preaching congregations is that seeking medical treatment for an illness is evidence of a lack of faith. Not every prosperity preacher believes medical treatment is against the will of God. In May of 1990, Betty Price, wife of Frederick K. C. Price (pastor of Crenshaw Christian Center in Los Angeles), was diagnosed with lymphoma. Lymphoma is a tumor in the lymphatic cells of the immune system. Rather than simply praying and believing God for healing, Betty Price underwent chemotherapy and radiation treatments. After the treatments, she had hip replacement surgery. Radiation treatments had damaged her hip socket so that her bones were rubbing against each other. In her book, *Through the Fire and Through the Water*, Betty Price recounts how she stood on the word of God while undergoing medical treatment. Despite the fact that she endured months of treatments before she was healed, she believed that she was healed even before beginning the treatments. The Prices received a lot of criticism from people in Word of Faith circles about undergoing medical treatment. In her book, Betty Price advises her readers to get help for their medical conditions as soon as they suspect they have a problem.

As Betty Price attests, rather than being a sign of weak faith, seeking medical treatment may be indicative of an all-encompassing faith—faith that is strong enough to believe that God's omnipotence is not limited to miraculous healing.

God also uses the gifts and talents of medical professionals whom God created and gifted to heal the people of God. Limiting the work of God to miraculous acts only is an attempt of humanity to confine God whose very nature defies and resists confinement of any sort.

Prosperity preachers teach their followers that if a person is not healed, something is wrong with that person's faith. Inherent in this position is the belief that sickness, disease, and death are punishment for ungodly behavior. We found when we looked at some Scripture passages that sickness and disease are not always punishment for wrongdoing. Sometimes the reasons why people were sick or experienced disease are unclear. Therefore, since sickness and disease are not always punishment, death may also not always be punishment.

In many of our traditions, including the Word of Faith movement, we are taught that Christians will be rewarded upon their deaths with life with Jesus. Promises of eternal life for the faithful are many: John 3:15; 5:39; 6:54, 68; 17:2; Acts 13:48; Romans 2:7; 5:21; 6:23; 1 Timothy 6:12,19. In John 14:2, Jesus told his disciples that he was going to prepare a place for them so that where he was going they could be there also. In Revelation 21:9-27, the New Jerusalem described by John (a city with twelve gates; walls of emerald, jasper, and sapphire; and streets of gold) is interpreted by many Christians as heaven. So on the one hand, by teaching people that death results from lack of faith, we teach that death is punishment. On the other hand, we teach that when we die in Christ, our reward for being good and faithful Christians is life with Jesus. If we truly believe that faithful Christians are rewarded upon their deaths with lives spent in eternity with Christ, why do we also teach that death is punishment?

Therefore, if the presence of sickness and disease is not always the result of sin in the Bible, we should rethink the connection between faith, healing, and death. Just as sickness and disease are not always punishment for sinful behavior, death may also not be punishment for lack of faith. We must always be aware that though God is omnipotent, omniscient, and omnipresent, God is also sovereign, meaning God will do what God wants to do. Perhaps a real act of faith is trusting that God knows what is best in particular situations and circumstances.

When preaching Isaiah 53:5 in the African American prophetic preaching tradition, the preacher could parallel the suffering servant in the text who suffered and lived his life trying to get the people of Judah to turn back to God with servants of God in our world who suffered. There are people in our contemporary world who lived their lives trying to get people in their own communities to stop oppressing others and embrace God's ways of justice and equality. An example of such suffering servants can be found in Anne and Carl Braden.

In 1954 in Shively, Kentucky, one couple demonstrated their willingness to combat racial prejudice and discrimination though the prospect of severe persecution was very high. A black couple, Andrew and Charlotte Wade, asked Carl and Anne Braden, a white couple whom they had met while working with the Progressive Party, to help them buy a home. The Wades had been repeatedly denied home loans for homes in white neighborhoods. They wanted the white couple, the Bradens, to purchase a home on their behalf, sign all of the mortgage documentation, and transfer the deed over to them. They, the Wades, would provide the money for the down payment. Carl and Anne Braden did not hesitate when they were asked. They signed the papers for the two-bedroom home and transferred the deed and the keys to the Wades.

The sale closed on Monday, May 10, 1954. By Thursday of that same week, all hell began to break loose. Crowds began to gather as neighbors realized that their new neighbors were black. A cross was burned in the field next to the Wades's new home, and gun shots were fired into their windows. People drove by—daily—shouting threats. Anne and Carl Braden were ostracized and verbally threatened by other whites. The legal battles left them financially broke and physically and emotionally weary. Anne had a miscarriage. Carl Braden was convicted of sedition (plotting to overthrow the government) and spent eight months in jail before charges were dropped.

Through it all, however, Anne believed in her heart that she and her husband had done the right thing, the only thing they could do. While growing up in Mississippi, she had been indoctrinated with the belief of white superiority. She had been taught never to call black men "sir" or black women "ladies"; *sir* and *ladies* were terms reserved for whites. But in college and after, she began to question racism. She met and talked to black people and began to work to right cultural wrongs. She believed her faith in Jesus Christ demanded it.[14]

Anne and Carl Braden are contemporary examples of suffering servants. There are many people in recent history and in our midst today who are willing to make personal sacrifices so that all people can be treated justly and with respect and dignity.

Prosperity preachers contend that Christians have a right to be healed. They also teach their followers that they are the righteousness of God. As the righteousness of God, they can claim to be spiritual equals with Jesus. This is the topic we'll explore in the next chapter.

NOTES

1. Bill Winston, "Jesus Healed Them All," http://bwmbroadcast.org/player/flash?stream=BW708a.mp4, accessed August 10, 2010.

2. E. W. Kenyon and Don Gossett Kenyon, *The Power of Your Words* (New Kensington, PA: Whitaker House, 1977), 96.

3. Ibid., 97.

4. E. W. Kenyon, *Jesus the Healer* (Lynnwood, WA: Kenyon's Gospel Publishing Society, 1940), 29.

5. Ibid.

6. Ibid., 38.

7. Ibid., 57.

8. Ibid.

9. Ibid., 14.

10. Ibid., 15.

11. Joel B. Green, Scot McKnight, and I. Howard Marshall, *Dictionary of Jesus and the Gospels* (Downers Grove, IL: InterVarsity, 1992), 301.

12. Paul Hanson, *Isaiah 40–66* (Louisville: John Knox, 1995), 156.

13. Mordecai Schreiber, "The Real 'Suffering Servant': Decoding a Controversial Passage in the Bible," *Jewish Bible Quarterly* 37, no. 1 (January–March 2009), 35–44.

14. Catherine Fosl, *Subversive Southerner: Anne Braden and the Struggle for Racial Justice in the Cold War South* (Lexington: University of Kentucky Press, 2006), 135–70.

CHAPTER 9

You Are the Righteousness of God

"You are the righteousness of God in Christ Jesus." This statement is frequently made by preachers of the prosperity gospel when they are trying to get believers to understand who they are in Christ and the rights and privileges to which they are entitled. In one sermon, Creflo Dollar cited E. W. Kenyon, who wrote that sin makes cowards of people because they will not stand up for their rights. Dollar contended that people do not stand up for their rights because of their sin consciousness. He asserted that Jesus was fearless in his ministry because he was righteous. Therefore, if believers can shed their sin consciousness, they will no longer be cowards and will then become the people God was calling them to be.

How many cowards do we have in the house? And how many days will we continue to be cowards? How many days will we continue to allow sin to make you a coward? Sin is not the problem. Jesus has already given an answer to sin. The blood has already taken care of sin. Sin is not the problem. Quit making sin the problem. We have an advocate with the Father. Sin is not the problem. And we have not only made it the problem, we've allowed it to make us the cowards. I'm not a coward. I have a right to everything he promised and declared in this book. Now I'm sorry that some people don't read all of it. But he has declared, he has declared I have a right to get answered prayer. He has declared that I have a right to come boldly to the throne of God. He has declared that I have a right to have forgiveness of my sin. He has declared that I have a right to be solid in every area, whole in every area of my life. And he has declared that I am to be rich. Now I am sorry that you don't want to stand up for that.[1]

Dollar was basically telling his hearers that the reason many of them do not claim their rights as the embodiment of the righteousness of God is because they are too scared to do so. They are supposed to go boldly to God and claim their rights. Their rights, according to Dollar, include being rich.

Bill Winston also tried to teach his hearers about the value of righteousness. In a sermon titled "Understanding Our Divinity," he told his hearers that when they were born again, "they assumed the same nature as God."[2] One of the struggles that new converts have is the renewing of their minds. Before receiving Christ, people live in condemnation. After receiving Christ, they live in righteousness.

Christians, Winston taught, have been programmed to believe that they have limits. But the new person who lives in righteousness is connected to the ability of God and therefore has no limits. Whereas people used to think small, after conversion they need to develop a new mentality. Winston cited Peter walking on the water as an example of a new mentality. When Peter saw Jesus walking on the water, he told Jesus to call out to him so he could walk on the water too. Undoubtedly, Winston speculated, there were people in the boat who were calling out to Peter, trying to get him to come back. They were telling him that he was crazy. But Peter believed that he could do what Jesus did. That "I can do anything" mentality is the mentality believers should have.

Both Dollar and Winston used Kenyon's teachings about the righteousness of God as the basis for their preaching. According to Kenyon, when Christ was resurrected from the grave, he gave Christians the ability to become the righteousness of God in him.[3] Righteousness is the ability to stand before God's presence as if one had never committed sin. Since believers have been declared righteous, they have God's own nature.[4]

Kenyon asserted that Christians no longer have to live with a sense of spiritual inferiority or with a constant sin consciousness; rather, believers should live with Son consciousness.[5] Son consciousness creates within believers the understanding that once they accept Jesus Christ as Lord of their lives, they have at work in them the same unlimited ability and wisdom of God as Christ has. Kenyon's Son consciousness is consistent with his teaching that believers are as much incarnations of God as Christ was when he was on earth.

According to Kenyon, God created human beings because of God's desire for fellowship. However, Adam's sin broke fellowship with God. Since the righteousness of humanity has been restored through Jesus, perfect fellowship between God and humanity can be restored if humanity allows sin consciousness to be eradicated.[6] If humanity does not allow sin consciousness to be eliminated, Satan's work in Adam will be proven more effective than God's work in Christ.[7] When believers realize they are the righteousness of God, they can take their places as sons and daughters of God and walk as fearlessly through life as Jesus did.[8]

The text these prosperity preachers cite as evidence is 2 Corinthians 5:21: "God made him who had no sin to be sin for us, so that in him we might become the righteousness of God" (NIV). Does being the righteousness of God mean that humanity actually assumes the very nature of God? Are Jesus and humans on equal footing in the eyes of God? Comparing Word of Faith theology to another mainline Protestant theology may be instructive.

Because of Christ's Righteousness Alone

John Calvin, one of the authors of Reformed theology and one of the theologians who emerged during the Protestant Reformation in the sixteenth century, can offer another theological perspective. Calvin wrote extensively in his *Institutes of the Christian Religion* about the justification by faith wherein humanity is forgiven of their sins and deemed righteous by God through their confession of faith in Jesus.[9] For Calvin, believers are deemed righteous because our mediator, Jesus, is righteous.

However, while Calvin believed that humans are made righteous in the eyes of God through Christ, he adamantly rejected the teachings of Andreas Osiander, a German theologian in his day, whom he contended was assigning divine attributes to humans. He argued that humans were not "transfused" with "divine essence" upon conversion.[10] While Kenyon believed that humans assumed God's nature when they were made righteous and were just as much incarnations of God as Christ, Calvin believed that being declared righteous was the beginning of a lifelong process of sanctification. Humans, according to Calvin, spent a lifetime living into their righteous status.

What was at stake for Calvin in making this distinction? Why spend so much time and effort on it? Calvin argued against humans being imbued with divinity when they were justified by faith because of the reality of sin. For Calvin, even though God declares humans to be righteous when they accept Christ, they are not free from sin. Christ was free from sin. Humans are declared righteous simply because of God's grace.[11] It was only by the grace of God, through the person and work of Jesus Christ, that humans receive salvation and justification. Calvin believed that the continued existence of sin, even among the converted, are a reality check for Christians that they are not as much incarnations of God as Christ.

While we should not allow the reality of our sinful natures to weigh us down, having some sin consciousness is not a bad thing. Being aware of sin and our propensity to commit sin allows us to be continually aware of dependency on God for all things. (I explore this further in Sifting the Wheat from the Chaff.)

The Favor of God

Calvin believed that serving God has benefits. One privilege of being the righteousness of God for Calvin is being the recipient of the favor of God. For Calvin, the favor of God is God's assurance of God's divine presence in this life and expectation of life with Christ in the next.[12] For Calvin the favor of God also includes God's blessings on human works (day-to-day activities) and work they do for God. Blessings on works represent divine favor, because by their own merit, human works do not measure up to divine standards. No matter how good human works are, they are still tarnished with sin. However, because God looks at human works through Jesus Christ, God is able to attribute to them value they ordinarily would not have.

Calvin argued that in as much as the promises of the law reward works, they are of little value, because the law is impossible for humans to fulfill. Though impossible to fulfill, the law still serves as a guide for godly living. However, when the promises of the gospel (which include free pardon of sins and being accepted by God) are substituted for the promises of the law, then God blessed the works of the faithful:

> But when the gospel promises are substituted, promises which announce the free pardon of sins, the result is not only that our persons are accepted of God, but his favor also is shown to our works, and that not only in respect that the Lord is pleased with them, but also because he visits them with the blessings which were due by agreement to the observance of his law. I admit,

therefore, that the works of the faithful are rewarded with the promises which God gave in his law to the cultivators of righteousness and holiness.[13]

While the favor of God for Calvin is given to the faithful according to the promises of God found in the law, godly favor does not necessarily equate to material wealth. Calvin believed that Christians can be faithful and blessed with the favor of God yet still be poor. For both prosperity theology and Calvin, the favor of God is a result of humanity being declared righteous by God. The difference between the two is that for prosperity theology, the favor of God manifests itself in the form of material wealth in addition to other blessings.

In one sermon, Jerry Savelle shared with his hearers that when he became a Christian in 1969, someone gave him a book by Bob Buess titled *Favor: The Road to Success*. Until Savelle read the book, he had no idea that God thought so highly of humanity. He had always been taught that human righteousness was as filthy rags before God. When he read the book, he discovered that God made humans a little lower than God-self and crowned them with glory and honor: "What is man, that thou art mindful of him? and the son of man, that thou visitest him? For thou hast made him a little lower than the angels, and hast crowned him with glory and honour" (Psalm 8:4-5, KJV).

Savelle also learned that God has favorable thoughts about men and women. Through favor, God ensures that Christians become winners rather than losers. He referred to Genesis 12:2 in which God told Abraham that he would make his name great to demonstrate God's promise to bless the people of God with divine favor. In Savelle's view, the favor of God and the grace of God are the same. While Savelle does not limit the favor of God to works associated with the law, he teaches that holiness and obedience to the word of God are necessary for believers to receive the blessings of

God. For Savelle, the favor of God includes entitlement to material wealth.

Savelle also teaches his followers that the favor of God will change rules, regulations, and policies if necessary.[14] He cited an example of a time in his own life when he and his wife were trying to enroll one of their daughters in school for the first time. According to state law, because of the date of her birth, his daughter had to wait an additional year before she could begin school. Savelle and his wife began to pray and declare divine favor. When it came time to enroll their daughter, the school official told Savelle that he did not understand what happened, but the law had changed and they were now able to enroll their daughter in school. Savelle declared this to be an example of God's divine favor at work in their lives. In the case of promotions at work, Savelle said that he knew people who did not have the seniority or the expertise that would qualify them for promotion. God nevertheless made a way for them to be promoted.

Sifting the Wheat from the Chaff

Bill Winston and other Word of Faith preachers tell their listeners that they are just as much incarnations of God as Jesus was. Indeed, when we examine John 14:12, we read that Jesus did tell the disciples that they would be able to do the same works (and even greater) than Jesus was able to do during his earthly ministry. However, as it relates to spiritual equality with Jesus, humanity still has to deal with the problem of sin. Therefore, humans are not Christ's spiritual equals.

Being recipients of the favor of God is especially good news for people who do not generally get much good news. People who struggle to meet their basic needs on a daily basis, who have been unemployed or underemployed for extended periods, and who don't know how they are going to pay the rent or mortgage are glad to hear that God will bless their lives if they live by the word of God. People who encounter discrimination in their workplaces based on race, ethnicity, or gender are overjoyed to hear that they can claim the favor of God to help them advance in the midst of opposition. These are the types of situations in which the favor of God is most needed. Having the assurance of God's blessings may help to give people in these circumstances the confidence they need to live boldly in the world and to dare to dream.

While it is good news to hear that God is able to work miracles on behalf of the people of God, Savelle's claims raise serious concerns. Christians who expect every law with which they take issue to be immediately changed and every regulation or policy that is disagreeable to them to be instantly eliminated are in for great disappointment. Even in cases of tremendous injustice, changing laws and policies can take months, years, decades, or even centuries. Chattel slavery of the West African–North American slave trade existed in this country for two hundred years before it was finally abolished. During that time, a lot of faithful Christians prayed, worked, and believed for its elimination. Even with all of that effort, it lasted for two centuries.

After the abolition of slavery in the United States, it took many more decades of prayer, pain, and protest to achieve legal equality for African Americans in the form of basic civil rights in the United States. For example, the Montgomery bus boycott alone, which began on December 1, 1955, to enable African Americans to ride in any section of the public bus system they chose, was a thirteen-month mass protest. Throughout that period, good Christian people were praying, walking, organizing, and sacrificing their time and efforts for the good of the cause. Many of these people had tremendous faith and believed God could do all things. Yet it took time to realize their dream of equality. The boycott ended with the United States Supreme Court ruling that segregation on public transportation was unconstitutional. It was just one of a series of protests launched over the years that ultimately culminated with civil rights being extended to African Americans. Though

God hears the prayers of God's people, sometimes the positive outcome of our prayers is not immediate.

As it relates to receiving promotions even though one is not qualified for the job, this too is problematic. First of all, people of God should always pray and ask God to reveal to them God's will for their lives. This means that though we may want a promotion, we should first discern whether the promotion we desire is in line with God's will for us. After discerning God's will, Christians should then pray for help to achieve the qualifications necessary to get the job. No one should want to work in a job for which she or he is not qualified. Not being qualified for a position sets people up for failure. We certainly want to start a job with all of the knowledge and skills necessary to do it well.

However, indiscriminate belief in the favor of God, in which one claims divine favor in all situations, such as getting a premium parking space, the best tickets to a football game, or moved to the front of a very long line can serve to turn our omnipotent, omniscient, and omnipresent God into our own personal valet—a God who is at our beck and call to make our lives more comfortable and eliminate any inconveniences we may encounter in our daily lives. God does not exist for our convenience. We exist to bring glory to God. God helps us to bring God glory by giving us everything we need to live happy, productive, fulfilling lives that are accountable to God in every way (spiritually, physically, emotionally, and mentally).

The favor of God can also be a license for mediocrity with the expectation that God will somehow bless even our feeblest, most token efforts. If we adopt this perception of godly favor, we believe that we no longer have to work hard to realize tangible results. We only have to pray and believe that God will work out situations on our behalf. For example, a medical student who prays for God's help to pass an exam for which he or she has not adequately prepared could claim God's divine favor to earn a passing grade. However, if that

student were enabled to pass without acquiring the necessary knowledge, that student would be robbing any future
patients of a physician who is truly competent in the profession. None of us would want to be the patient of a doctor
who relied on divine favor to get through medical school.
None of us would want to be operated on by a surgeon who
did not quite master the breadth of knowledge necessary to
be an excellent surgeon. We want doctors who worked hard,
studied diligently, and gained the knowledge and skills necessary to treat us effectively. Just as we have high expectations
of our physicians, we should also have high expectations of
ourselves and all people. We should always strive to do the
best we can in every aspect of our lives. God will help us, but
we must also do our part. God will be there when we need
God most.

Among other issues raised in this chapter, I examined the
concept of divine favor. Divine favor is good news for people
who have been and are being treated unjustly in any way.
African Americans are intimately acquainted with injustice,
especially as it pertains to race. Yet, in the next chapter, we
discover that Creflo Dollar contends that race does not matter.

NOTES

1. Creflo Dollar Jr., "Ruling and Reigning through Righteousness," Creflo Dollar Ministries, 2001, audiocassette.

2. Bill Winston, "Understanding Our Divinity," http://bwmbroadcast.
org/player/flash?stream=BW591_2.mp4 (accessed September 17, 2010).

3. E. W. Kenyon, *Jesus the Healer* (Lynnwood, WA: Kenyon's Gospel
Publishing Society, 1940), 8–9. By "righteousness of God," Kenyon means
a state of being without sin before God. At the moment the believer accepts
Christ as Savior, he or she is declared righteous.

4. Ibid.

5. E. W. Kenyon, *Identification: A Romance in Redemption* (Lynnwood,
WA: Kenyon's Gospel Publishing Society, 1941), 49–50.

6. E. W. Kenyon, *The Father and His Family: The Story of Man's Redemption* (Lynnwood, WA: Kenyon's Gospel Publishing Society, 1937),
219.

7. Ibid., 220.

8. Ibid., 223.

9. John Calvin, *Institutes of the Christian Religion*, 3.11.2, Christian Classics Ethereal Library, 2002, www.ntslibrary.com/PDF%20Books/Calvin%20Institutes%20of%20Christian%20Religion.pdf (accessed December 13, 2011).

10. Ibid., 3.11.5.

11. Ibid., 3.11.11.

12. Ibid., 3.2.28.

13. Ibid., 3.17.3.

14. Jerry Savelle, "The Favor of God #2." Jerry Savelle Ministries video podcast, iTunes, downloaded October 6, 2011.

CHAPTER 10

Race Doesn't Matter

While sitting in the sanctuary of World Changers Church International in College Park, Georgia, in 2007, I became keenly aware of two things: I was worshipping in a black church—and yet I wasn't. Almost all of the people around me were African American. The soulful, dynamic, and rhythmic music shared by the praise team was similar to music heard in African American congregations around the country. The preaching of Creflo Dollar himself often echoed the rhetorical cadences and passion of African American preachers throughout the African diaspora. The call and response interactions between Dollar and the congregation were energizing and unceasing. My neighbors clapped, stood, danced, and shouted when the Spirit led them. I was experiencing African American worship and preaching.

At the same time, the presence of television cameras reminded me that Dollar's congregation did not consist merely of the eight or nine thousand people who attended the eleven o'clock worship service that Sunday, but also the millions of people of many different races, ethnicities, cultures, and traditions who would watch the sermon (and only the sermon) on the church's website or on iTunes, hear it through podcast, or order the DVD version. The bifurcated reality of worship at World Changers Church International reflects Creflo Dollar's ambiguous relationship to race: he knows it exists, even embodies cultural mores associated with people of African American descent, but insists that race is unimportant for Christian people to acknowledge and understand. Why? Before we attempt to understand Dollar's perspective on race, it is important to understand who Dollar is and a bit about his journey.

Dollar's Journey

Creflo Dollar Jr. is the son of the late Creflo Dollar Sr., one of the first black police officers in College Park, Georgia, and Emma Dollar, former worker in the Kathleen Mitchell Elementary school cafeteria, also in College Park. Dollar was the first black student to attend Kathleen Mitchell, a school where he would later host his own church. He played linebacker at Lakeshore High School and also served as the student government president.[1] One person who attended high school with Dollar claims that "[Dollar] was not religious by any stretch of the imagination, but he was a good guy."[2]

Dollar did not accept Christ until his freshman year in college. Upon entering college, his plan was to become a professional football player. "God, however, had a different course for my life. I ended up getting injured and sitting on the bench for much of my college career."[3] While studying education at West Georgia College in Carrollton, Georgia, Dollar and his roommate began conducting a Bible study in their room.[4] The Bible study became very popular and was soon attracting over a hundred people. Dollar called the Bible study World Changers Bible Study.[5] Dollar also met his wife, Taffi, at the college.

In 1984 Dollar graduated from West Georgia College with a bachelor's degree in education. After graduation, he worked as a teen counselor at the Brawner Psychiatric Institute in Atlanta.[6] In 1986[7] Dollar founded World Changers Ministries Christian Center, which first gathered in the Kathleen Mitchell Elementary School with eight people.[8] After two years of meeting in the cafeteria, the ministry negotiated for and purchased property that formerly housed the Atlanta Christian Center Church in College Park. Soon after moving into the new church, the ministry added a weekly radio broadcast and four services each Sunday to accommodate its growing membership.

Today World Changers Church International has a membership of more than twenty thousand, a number that does not include members at World Changers Church–New York, and World Changers Church–Español. Dollar serves as the chief executive officer of World Changers Ministries, which he founded in 1986, also in College Park.

The preaching that sets Dollar apart, that defines his ministry and attracts millions of viewers to his broadcasts on television stations around the world, is his preaching about money. Were it not for his message of financial prosperity, he would be just another charismatic preacher. His message of prosperity has set him apart by his sheer audacity to claim that God wants Christians to be rich. However, while admonishing his listeners to follow the word of God and become wealthy, Dollar dissuades them from acknowledging the existence of racism. Let us examine his views on race.

Dollar, Preaching, and Race

In his book *The Color of Love*, Dollar addresses the issue of racism. For Dollar, racism is a spirit of division that manifests itself in the form of conflict when one race rises up against another race.[9] He is very clear that he is not writing to address the existence of racism in the world in general, but in the church in particular.[10] Dollar is not concerned about racism outside of the church, because "in the eyes of God, there are only two races: believers and unbelievers."[11]

In his argument, Dollar makes the mistake of equating the Greek word *ethnos* with *race*: "Ethnos means a race, a tribe, a non-Jewish one, a Gentile." As a result, Dollar takes Matthew to mean "Race shall rise up against race." Therefore, according to Dollar, racism was predicted in the biblical text.

Dollar's failure to distinguish between ethnicity and race betrays his ignorance of how and why race was constructed in the seventeenth century in the United States as a way of justifying the enslavement of Africans and to "preserve the distinctiveness of the Black/white dichotomy."[12] Before the advent of race, people were identified by *ethnos* or ethnicity. Ethnicity refers to groups of people who share cultural traits, such as language, religion, geographic location and place of origin, traditions, values, beliefs, and food preferences.[13] In the seventeenth century, race became the paradigm for instituting and preserving the social reality of inequality as a naturally occurring phenomenon and a product of human biological differences, such as skin color, hair texture, eye shape, etc.[14] Racial categorization was adopted by American colonies at the turn of the eighteenth century as a way of justifying the enslavement of Africans. According to racial ideology, biological differences between whites and Africans made ranking races necessary. Naturally, people of African descent occupied the lowest level of the hierarchy.[15] Racial ideology became a means of restricting access to privilege, power, and wealth.[16] Therefore, racism can be defined as "the practice of discrimination and prejudice based on racial classification supported by the power to enforce that prejudice."[17] According to this definition, racism is by definition systemic. Race as ideology without the power to enforce discrimination and prejudice is only an idea. Racism puts racial ideology into practice.

In *The Color of Love*, Dollar asserts that people no longer need to identify with their *natural heritage* once they are born again, because they have a new *spiritual heritage* with which to identify.[18] When believers identify with their new spiritual heritage, they can create their own realities in which racism is no longer an issue. Dollar cites 1 Corinthians 1:11-13 as Paul's critique on racial identification: "For it hath been declared unto me of you, my brethren, by them which are of the house of Chloe, that there are contentions among you. Now this I say, that every one of you saith, I am of Paul; and I of Apollos; and I of Cephas; and I of Christ. Is Christ divided? Was Paul crucified for you? or were ye baptized in the name of Paul?" (KJV).

For most people (including biblical scholars) reading this text, Paul was urging Corinthian believers not to take sides and divide themselves according to which apostle converted them. Rather, they should identify with Christ, the one about whom all of the apostles preached. Dollar has a different interpretation of the text. He believes that Paul was admonishing the people to no longer identify with their *natural heritage*. Notwithstanding the problems with interpretation, identifying with one's *natural heritage* for Dollar is no longer necessary after one converts to Christianity.

In his book, Dollar critiques those who try to discover the ethnic and or racial identities of people in the Bible or who espouse black images of Jesus. For Dollar, those people are creating division in the church. To the people who believe that knowing the ethnic identity of people in the Bible could help some people build self-esteem, Dollar wrote, "They need to get saved." In other words, the problem of self-esteem can be resolved once people know who they are in Christ Jesus.

One consequence of racism in the church for Dollar is the cessation of *increase*.[19] By *increase*, Dollar means blessings of God that are manifested in the lives of believers, such as physical health and financial prosperity. When divisions such as those caused by racism exist, God is not able to bless individuals or ministries as much as God would like. For Dollar, the solution to racism in the church is forgiveness and reconciliation:

If you are white, I want you to go to a black person. I want you to look that person square in the eyes, then I want you to repent and to apologize for the sins of your ancestors against black people. Be willing to say from your heart, "I am sorry."

If you are black, I want you to go to a white person. I want you to look that person square in the eyes, then I want you to repent for the years of unforgiveness towards white people that you have carried in your heart.

If you, as a believer, have had feelings of hate, distrust, or hostility towards people of any other race, it's vitally important that you go to some member of that race and repent of those feelings.[20]

Dollar expects repentance (admitting one's transgressions, asking for forgiveness, changing one's attitude and behaviors) to lead to reconciliation (mending of relationships). It seems that Dollar has adopted the views of repentance found in the teachings of many white evangelical Christian churches and parachurch organizations, such as InterVarsity Christian Fellowship and Promise Keepers, an evangelical Christian men's movement. In some Promise Keepers events, men are encouraged to go to their brothers of another race and confess the prejudice they harbor in their hearts and ask for forgiveness.[21] Often these confessions are laced with tears and hugs. While the hugs and tears may reflect sincere sorrow and regret, repentance without concrete action on all levels can leave intact the racist systems and structures that continue to negatively affect the lives of blacks and other minorities. Dollar seems to have embraced a worldview held by some white evangelicals that renders him incapable of a more critical analysis of racial issues.[22]

Three aspects of this uncritical worldview are the beliefs that (1) individuals exist independently of institutions (have free will and are individually accountable for their own actions); (2) relationships with Christ and healthy relationships with family, friends, and other church members help Christians to make the right choices in life; and (3) sin is limited to individuals. These aspects are known respectively as *account-able freewill individualism*, *relationalism*, and *antistructural-ism*. The common thread in each of these aspects is belief that individuals always act independently of human systems and of traditional ways of thinking. Dollar's directive to his fol-lowers to combat racism in the church by apologizing to and receiving apologies from people of a different race is evidence of his inability to recognize the systemic nature of racism, even in the institutional church. Individual regret does not automatically result in changes in the traditional ways that officers are elected, evangelism is implemented, budget allot-ments are determined, and hiring decisions are made.

Dollar's lack of concern for the existence of racism out-side of the church is indicative of his belief that the most influential relationships that Christians have in their lives are with Christ, family, and other Christians. While these rela-tionships undoubtedly influence our thinking and are vital to our emotional and spiritual well-being, they too are part of a larger web of influences that each of us experiences in our daily lives. Webs of influence include local organizations, such as schools, universities and colleges, chambers of com-merce, city governments, retail outlets, local businesses, local and national news programs, social media, favorite websites, television, and radio. Each of these entities operates with its own set of biases and prejudices that are often transferred to those who avail themselves of their services. For example, if Christians hear on their favorite radio station that their unemployment is caused by illegal immigration of Mexicans into the United States, they may choose to believe it and be-gin to discriminate against and even hate all Mexicans. Their church may teach love, but the radio station teaches hate. Christians are influenced by many different entities.

Dollar's call for individual confession of racism attests to his belief that sin itself is limited to individuals. This belief denies the existence of corporate sin that impacts large seg-ments of society. While not inherently racist, payday lending is an example of corporate sin. Payday loans are small loans ranging from $100 to $1,000, depending on state regulations, made by independent lenders to people who find themselves in financial emergencies. Generally the loans are made to meet expenses until the client receives her or his next paycheck. The sin of payday loans is the exorbitant finance charges that clients must pay to receive them. For example, one lender, Check into Cash, charges a $15 fee on a $100 fourteen-day loan, which is the equivalent of an annual percentage rate of 391 percent.[23] In Exodus 22:25 God forbade Israelites to charge interest on loans they made to the poor. Though charging interest on all loans is common practice today, triple-digit annual percentage rates are oppressive and debilitating. Though payday lending is legal, it is sinful at a corporate level.

Dollar and Hurricane Katrina

The headquarters for Creflo Dollar's World Changers Church International is located about five hundred miles north of New Orleans, Louisiana. During the week of August 29, 2005, hurricane Katrina hit the Gulf Coast leaving thousands homeless and hundreds of people dead and missing. Katrina was the most devastating storm in US history. According to one CBS News report, 75 percent of the areas devastated by Katrina in the city of New Orleans were populated by black people.[24] This report also communicated that the odds of living in damaged areas were greater for blacks, renters, and poor people.[25] In the days and weeks following Katrina, people across the nation were horrified by the lack of response of city, state, and national agencies to the needs of people on the Gulf Coast. US citizens everywhere were demanding to know why the people had not been assisted in a timely fashion.

The president of Jefferson Parish in New Orleans, Aaron Broussard, was literally in tears on *Meet the Press* on Sunday, September 4, 2005, when he told the story of a mother who had drowned in New Orleans because she received no help.

Broussard repeated over and over again, "Nobody's coming to get us! Nobody's coming to get us!"

On the same Sunday on which Broussard made this passionate appeal, Dollar's broadcast sermon was titled "Levels of the Anointing, Part 1."[26] In this sermon, not only did Dollar not critique the neglect of the people on the Gulf Coast, but he did not even mention that Katrina had taken place. He used Psalm 4 as his opening Scripture. In Psalm 4 the writer praises God for bringing him out of a desolate pit and setting his feet upon a rock where he was now secure. Dollar interpreted the text as saying that the hearers cannot allow their circumstances to keep them down.

It is likely that this sermon was scheduled for broadcast before Katrina devastated the Gulf Coast. However, some ministry broadcasts, such as T. D. Jakes's *Potter's House*, edited their regular broadcast to insert footage about their ministry's responses to Katrina and offer prayers for the victims. Creflo Dollar and the *Changing Your World* broadcast remained silent. Even on broadcasts in the weeks following Katrina, Dollar made no mention of the tragedy.

In the days following Katrina, Dollar accepted an invitation to the White House to meet with President Bush along with other religious leaders. The purpose of the meeting was to strategize about responses to Katrina. It is ironic that though Dollar omitted any mention of the tragedy from his broadcasts, he was sought by the White House to work with other leaders to work out a plan to meet the needs of the victims. Preaching has been an avenue of pastors and faith leaders for centuries to raise awareness of social and political issues and to mobilize congregants to take action. Dollar chose not to use this particular strategy though the organized efforts of his millions of followers could have made a tremendous impact. World Changers Church International undoubtedly provided aid to Katrina victims. However, Dollar missed an opportunity to multiply the breadth and depth of his impact exponentially by failing to rally his listeners.

Sifting the Wheat from the Chaff

In an ideal world, Creflo Dollar would be correct about his presumption that race does not matter. After all, race was socially constructed to privilege whites over blacks and other people of color. The ideology of race is only real insofar as people adopt it, live their lives according to it, and build institutions around it. Nevertheless, racial ideology is indelibly woven into the fabric of our society to such an extent that no sector has remained untainted by it—not even the church. Unfortunately, Dollar's failure to acknowledge the existence of racism does not change the fact that his hearers may be victims. As victims of racism, listeners' self-esteem may be impacted even though they know who they are in Christ. And although Dollar's listeners may be saved, sanctified, and filled with the Holy Spirit, they still may be greeted with barriers when they try to access goods and services in the public square.

Dollar, born in 1963, grew up in the years after many civil rights battles had been waged and won. Thanks to the *Brown v. Board of Education* Supreme Court decision of 1954 and subsequent state and local enforcement, segregation in public schools was ruled unconstitutional, making it possible for Dollar to become the first black student to attend the Kathleen Mitchell Elementary School in College Park. Thanks to the Civil Rights Act of 1964, which outlawed race-based and other types of discrimination, Dollar is able to purchase air time to broadcast his television program, purchase land, and build a church wherever he wishes. He can live in any neighborhood he can afford.

On a daily basis, Dollar takes full advantage of the opportunities that the hard-fought civil rights victories of his ancestors have afforded him. Yet he chooses to publicly adopt the uncritical and limited beliefs of some white evangelicals who deny the existence of systemic sin. Racism is not a personal problem. By definition, racism is systemic because it requires the power of social structures to enforce its ideology. Racism is a systemic structure that must be methodically and intentionally dismantled. Individual confession and repentance are only a small part of the dismantling process. The laws and socially accepted behaviors that enforce racial ideology must be denounced and repealed.

Though Dollar has been the focus of this critique on race, his views on race are representative of prosperity preachers in general. The decision of prosperity preachers to adopt white evangelical mores in their preaching has far-reaching implications because of the range of their influence. People who watch and internalize prosperity preaching take the theology into their churches. As a result, prosperity preaching influences not just people in other Word of Faith churches but also large and small churches of various denominations. If African American churches in particular and Christian churches in general begin to deny the existence of racism, many social injustices will go unchecked, unacknowledged, and unaddressed. For many people, African American churches have been their primary witnesses in speaking out and working against their oppression based on race. What will become of racially oppressed people if African American churches cease to bear prophetic witness against racism?

Many prosperity preachers ignore racism outside of the church. They choose instead to highlight and address issues related to race in the church by admonishing their followers to make personal confessions. Just as prosperity preachers teach their people that racism in the church can be eliminated through personal confession, they also believe that the key to eliminating all social sin is personal conversion of the entire nation, one person at a time. We'll look at that topic in chapter 11.

NOTES

1. John Blake, "Pastors Choose Sides over Direction of Black Church," *Atlanta Journal-Constitution*, February 15, 2005.

2. Ibid.

3. "Dr. Creflo A. Dollar Biography," World Changers Church, New York, http://www.worldchangerschurchnewyork.org/bio_t.aspx (accessed October 29, 2011).

4. Ibid.

5. Ibid.

6. Blake, "Pastors Choose Sides."

7. In the same year that Dollar started the World Changers Ministries, his parents divorced. The divorce came one year after Creflo Dollar Sr. was sued by a fellow police officer for deliberately shooting him. Officer L. Kendall Hall sued Dollar Sr. and the city of College Park. The lawsuit was settled out of court. See ibid.

8. Jean Gordon, "Dollar Brings Popular Prosperity Gospel to City," *Clarion Ledger*, May 13, 2006.

9. Creflo Dollar Jr., *The Color of Love: Understanding God's Answer to Racism, Separation and Division* (Tulsa: Harrison House, 1997), 16.

10. Ibid., 6.

11. Ibid., 49.

12. Audrey Smedley and Brian D. Smedley, "Race as Biology Is Fiction, Racism as a Social Problem Is Real," *American Psychologist* 60, no. 1 (2005): 20.

13. Ibid., 17.

14. Ibid.

15. Ibid., 20.

16. Ibid., 22.

17. National Association of Social Workers, "Institutional Racism and the Social Work Profession: A Call to Action," 2007, http://www.socialworkers.org/diversity/InstitutionalRacism.pdf (accessed October 27, 2011), 6.

18. By "natural heritage," Dollar means racial or ethnic heritage.

19. Dollar, *The Color of Love*, 241.

20. Ibid., 264.

21. Michael O. Emerson and Christian Smith, *Divided by Faith: Evangelical Religion and the Problem of Race in America* (New York: Oxford University Press, 2000), 66–68.

22. Ibid., 76–80.

23. "What Else Should I Know about Payday Loans?" Check into Cash, http://www.checkintocash.com/how-it-works.htm (accessed October 27, 2011).

24. Elliott Stonecipher, "Study: The New Orleans Population in Peril," CBS News, January 27, 2006, http://www.cbsnews.com/stories/2006/01/27/katrina/main1247418.shtml (accessed February 18, 2006).

25. Ibid.

26. Creflo Dollar, "Levels of the Anointing, Part I," http://interactive.creflodollarministries.org/broadcasts/archives2005_t.asp?site=CDM (accessed February 18, 2006).

CHAPTER 11

Living by the Word of God Eliminates Social Ills

"If people would make a decision to live their lives by the principles of the Word of God, all of the social ills in our society would cease to exist."[1] These are the words of Creflo Dollar in a 2005 interview with the *Atlanta Journal Constitution*. The focus of the article, which was published during Black History Month, was the future of the black church. Citing the title of Martin Luther King's book *Where Do We Go from Here?* as a point of reference, the article contended that black church leaders were locked in a bitter debate about the black church's mission.[2] Some leaders felt that parts of the church were abandoning their prophetic core "by no longer confronting political or economic institutions of power." Others believed they were extending King's ministry by "emphasizing issues such as economic empowerment."

By his remarks to the interviewer, Dollar fit in the latter category. He asserted that the divine economy was a means of debt cancellation. Since God recompenses believers multifold for the money they donate to people and churches, the divine economy yields the best return on investment anyone can get.[3] Believers can use their returns to pay off their debts. Though he argued that his ministry also helps people achieve freedom, he admitted that his approach was very different from King's: "Rather than focus on what's wrong with our society, we choose to focus on sharing the gospel of Jesus Christ with every person we possibly can. . . . If people would make a decision to live their lives by the principles of the Word of God, all of the social ills in our society would cease to exist."[4]

Dollar was correct when he implied that King and other prophetic preachers focused on what was wrong with *society*. While Dollar and other prosperity preachers focus on individuals, many prophetic preachers are more communal. Prosperity preachers seek to affect social reform indirectly through individual conversion to faith. They believe that once people are converted, they will live according to the word of God. When converts live according to the word of God, the world will better reflect the will of God.

Prophetic preachers prefer to affect social reform directly. They highlight injustice being perpetrated against particular populations or communities and call for reform of systemic structures, laws, and practices to make people's lives better. By calling for and working toward communal reform, prophetic preachers hold politicians accountable to truly act in the best interests of the people they are elected to serve. They hold institutions, corporations, and ecclesial bodies accountable to live into the best of their ideals. They also hold individuals accountable to live according to the word of God. By holding all segments of society accountable, prophetic preachers are acting in accordance with godly mandates communicated by prophets to the people of Israel in the Old Testament, the Hebrew Bible.

The risk of focusing on individual reform versus communal accountability is that people may not act outside of their own best interests—especially when they are taught that they are entitled by God to be rich and to enjoy godly favor.

Whether the topic is money, the anointing, physical healing, or the righteousness of God, prosperity preaching encourages hearers to seek God's blessings for themselves as individuals and for their families. The individualistic nature of prosperity preaching is exemplified in one sermon in which Dollar instructs his hearers to make confessions. As we explored in chapter 8, confessions are petitions or series of definitive statements (usually made audibly) detailing needs, wants, and desires believers expect God to grant them. In this sermon, Dollar informs his hearers that they should compose their confessions based on the word of God:

> We cannot receive the product of a thing until we understand the process of how to get it. And so what we're doing now, and this is a faith life, so I'm documenting what I'm believing God for. I'm not going to be saying, "Lord, I'm thankful that I have money to pay the light bill this month." No! My confession will not be that. My confession will be:
>
>> Father, I will never be in lack again.
>> And whatever I need, there is sufficiency in all things.
>> And I am a millionaire.
>> And I have more money than any bank in this natural world can hold.
>> And Father, my body is tremendously healed.
>> My family is free from tragedy. I won't ever have to worry about tragedy.
>> No plane will crash on me, and if it does, I will be the one to survive.
>> And all of these things that I am setting in place right now.
>
> See, instead of waiting until the devil comes to put him on the run, put him on the run right now.[5]

In Dollar's confession, he and his family are the beneficiaries of God's blessings. Therefore, when God honors Dollar's confessions, *Dollar's* needs will be met. *Dollar* will be a millionaire (he already is). *Dollar* and *his* family will be free from tragedy and so on. One question that comes to mind is, "If Dollar truly believes God will grant all petitions believers make that are in accord with the word of God, then why does he only teach believers to pray for themselves?"

Would it not be ideal for believers to access the power of God not just for themselves and their families, but for everyone? Why would they not pray that God provide money, food, and shelter for all of the poor people of the world? Why does Dollar instruct the hearers to confess that if a plane crashes that they, as individuals will be the only ones to survive? Can they not just as easily petition God for the survival of everyone on the plane?

Perhaps the reason adherents of the Word of Faith movement are not instructed to make confessions on behalf of others is because of a sense of *Christian entitlement*, the belief that only those who choose to follow particular teachings of Christ are entitled to receive certain benefits. Those who choose not to believe get what they deserve. A sense of Christian entitlement sees no need to pursue social justice issues. If everyone would simply follow Christ, all social justice issues would disappear. Those with a sense of Christian entitlement believe that non-Christians, and other Christians who do not believe as they do, do not deserve benefits.

This sense of Christian entitlement distorts the example that Christ lived for us. Jesus expressed an unconditional love for *all* people. When people were hungry in the Bible, Jesus fed them. He did not just feed people who believed or lived in a particular way. When Jesus healed the sick, he healed them all. When Jesus preached in the synagogue in Luke 4 that he had come to set free the captive and liberate the oppressed, he did not stipulate that he would help only those who believed as he wanted them to.

Perhaps one of the reasons the sense of Christian entitlement exists is because believers feel they deserve blessings because of all of the seeds they are sowing, confessions they are making, lives they are living, CDs and DVDs they are buying. These believers are working hard and investing time and resources into being good Christians. Why should others who are not living godly lives be the beneficiaries of God's blessings? If others want to be blessed, then they, too, can follow the advice prescribed by Word of Faith preachers or other Christian ministries.

For African Americans and other people who have felt disenfranchised and marginalized by society, Christian entitlement may be good news. To believe that God has a special place in God's heart for them is a welcome change from being forgotten and neglected. However, Christian entitlement is just as dangerous as any other type of entitlement. To believe that one is the exception is to forget God's second greatest commandment: "Thou shalt love thy neighbour as thyself" (Mark 12:31, KJV). This commandment reminds us that the goodness we want for ourselves is the same goodness we should want for our neighbors. *Neighbors* is an all-inclusive term that refers to all humanity. Therefore, just as we do not want to be the victims of injustice, we should not sit idly by and watch others be victimized—even if they are not Christians.

In contrast with prosperity theology, black prophetic preachers remind us all that God's people are called to be a justice-seeking people. But is black prophetic preaching still needed in the twenty-first century? Or have the issues that made it necessary in the past been fully resolved? Let us examine the current state of black America and determine roles for both prosperity gospel and black prophetic preaching.

State of Black America in 2010

There is an old saying that by the time America gets a cold, African Americans have pneumonia. According to statistics published in 2010 by the National Urban League, this saying is still true. Unemployment rates are 14.8 percent for blacks and 8.5 percent for whites. Less than half of black families own homes versus 75 percent of whites. Disparities in economic opportunity are mirrored in health care statistics, where 19.1 percent of blacks are without health insurance versus 10.8 percent of whites. Among black children ages six to eleven, 18.6 percent of boys and 24 percent of girls are overweight. For white children, the corresponding numbers are 15.5 percent for boys and 14.4 percent for girls. For people older than twenty-five years old, whites are one and a half times more likely to hold a bachelor's degree than blacks. High school dropout rates are 13 percent for blacks and 10.8 percent for whites. Blacks are six times more likely to be incarcerated than whites.

Causes for these disparities are many.[6] Much is accounted for by systemic injustices that still exist in various segments of societies. Personal accountability is an important factor as well. Black America has not yet overcome.

Strengths and Shortcomings of Prosperity versus Prophetic Preaching

While prosperity preaching has many shortcomings, it also has strengths that are beneficial to the well-being of all people. First of all, prosperity theology emphasizes the need for personal accountability in the lives of believers. By preaching that believers must follow the word of God in their daily lives in order to receive the benefits of God, prosperity preachers remind their people that actions have consequences. If they want to experience the goodness of God, they must be faithful to God.

Prosperity theology also reminds believers that they do have the ability to control their fates. Prosperity preachers teach their people they have a chest full of godly tools from which they can draw to live blessed lives: the anointing, status as the righteousness of God, and faith in the omnipotence of God. The most prolific tool is the unwavering belief that God is able to do all things.

In Milmon Harrison's *Righteous Riches*, a sociological study of a Word of Faith congregation in Sacramento, California, he found that some people felt that prosperity gospel helped them feel empowered, able to take control of their lives rather than have the circumstances of their lives control them. The young woman quoted below had formerly been a member of a Methodist church. She was asked what teaching convinced her to become a member of a Word of Faith church:

> For me, as an African American woman, I felt like I was no longer put in a box. You know, I didn't have to do things because I was African American. Or, I was not limited simply because I was African American. I was a child of God first who happened to be African American. And that broadened my knowledge base; it broadened my desires. I didn't feel limited anymore; I didn't feel limited by the color of my skin. I shouldn't say simply by the color of my skin, but by the people's stereotypical views of me as an African American woman. I was no longer concerned with the images that other people had about me. Because I now knew how God thought of me, and that was more important than anything. And so, I think that was the key thing, for me, that kept me there. I wasn't in this "what The Man does to you," you know, The White Man—it wasn't about that. It was about my relationship with God and what God has promised me, and me saying I'm going to live those promises. So it was getting me out of that box, that limited thinking.[7]

This young woman found the message of prosperity theology affirming of her as a person. God did not care about her race, and her church was not focused on what the white man does to black people. She found comfort in knowing that she could, through the power of God, control her own life.

This strength of prosperity gospel is also a critique of some black prophetic preaching. While black prophetic preaching highlights what is wrong with society, it can take blaming "the

Man" and systemic structures to such an extreme that personal accountability becomes nonexistent. In this respect, black prophetic preachers can learn from prosperity preachers.

Conversely, prosperity preachers can learn much from black prophetic preachers. Black prophetic preachers, including some evangelicals, agree that social ills of society do not disappear automatically when people convert to Christianity. Prosperity preachers need only examine the social interactions of the converted Christians in their own congregations to disprove their theory that individual conversion yields social perfection. While many people inside churches profess Jesus Christ as their Savior, lying, cheating, backbiting, power grabbing, adultery, domestic abuse, racism/ethnocentrism, ageism, and classism exist among the saints of God. Christians strive to be like Jesus, but we fall short of Jesus' example every day. As long as humanity embodies flesh, we will need to intentionally address issues of social justice.

Christians are members of the body of Christ. That means that those of us who purport to follow Jesus are the hands, feet, eyes, and ears of Christ in the world. We should not only believe that Jesus is the Son of God and through him we have been given the gift of salvation, but we should also work to embody the salvation of which we are beneficiaries by being a justice-seeking people.

Jesus was ultimately crucified for being a social and political threat.[8] He proclaimed a kingdom of God in which the poor, the hungry, the distressed, the hated, and the excluded are called blessed. In the same kingdom, the rich, the full, the laughing ones, and those of good repute are forewarned of ill-fated futures. In the kingdom of God as articulated by Jesus, poverty is no longer a life sentence to marginalization and condemnation (by God or humans). Wealth is no longer a sign of godly favor or divine sanction. In the radical kingdom that Jesus proclaimed, blessings are directly dependent on human interaction and the degree to which those interactions embody God's kingdom. Jesus sought to liberate humanity from its self-made systems of power and privilege. As the body of Christ, we must be about his work every day of our lives.

NOTES

1. John Blake, "Pastors Choose Sides over Direction of Black Church," *Atlanta Journal Constitution*, February 15, 2005.

2. Ibid.

3. Creflo Dollar Jr., "No More Debt," Creflo Dollar Ministries, 2000, compact disc.

4. Blake, "Pastors Choose Sides."

5. Creflo Dollar Jr., "Christ in You, the Hope of Glory," pt. 1, 2006, Creflo Dollar Ministries, compact disc.

6. National Urban League, "The State of Black America 2010: Jobs: Responding to the Crisis," www.thechicagourbanleague.org/723210130204959623/lib/723210130204959623/EXECUTIVE%20SUMMARY%20StateBlkAmerica.pdf (accessed September 20, 2010).

7. Milmon F. Harrison, *Righteous Riches: The Word of Faith Movement in Contemporary African American Religion* (New York: Oxford University Press, 2005), 26.

8. Joel B. Green, Scot McKnight, and I. Howard Marshall, *Dictionary of Jesus and the Gospels* (Downers Grove, IL: InterVarsity, 1992), 154.

CHAPTER 12

Affirmations, Denouncements, and Reconstruction of Faith

Throughout this project I have critiqued prosperity theology on many levels. I have also attempted to affirm the gifts that this theology gives to the world in general and to Christianity in particular. The most significant gift the prosperity gospel gives is the gift of faith. In every prosperity sermon, listeners are taught to believe in a God who can do all things. They are taught that if they believe and do not doubt God's ability, nothing is impossible for them. This unshakable, immovable kind of faith plays a vital role in sustaining and edifying all people, but especially people who may have few things in life on which they can rely.

Faith, in turn, provides its own gifts. One of the gifts of faith is hope. Hope for a more abundant life compels people who listen to prosperity sermons to pray and believe for a tomorrow that is better and more reflective of God's grace than today.

Heightened awareness of personal accountability is also a gift that the prosperity gospel contributes to Christendom. Prosperity sermons admonish believers to live righteous lives—lives that are pleasing to God. Personal accountability includes having active prayer lives, reading the Bible daily, attending church regularly, being faithful in marriage, and tithing and giving offerings to a local congregation.

Like Pentecostal and Holiness traditions, prosperity theology reminds all Christians of the importance of the Holy Spirit in the daily lives of those who profess Christ. In prosperity theology, believers are taught that the Holy Spirit teaches, comforts, and most of all empowers them to do the work of ministry.

Denouncements

While faith, hope, personal accountability, and the empowerment of the Holy Spirit are gifts of the prosperity gospel, each of these gifts is accompanied by one primary shortcoming—they are taught as means of becoming rich. Adherents are taught to have faith in God so God will bless them with wealth. The better day they are taught to hope for is fraught with dreams of material wealth, including luxury cars, designer clothes, large homes, and unlimited amounts of cash. They are taught to live righteously so that God will make them rich. They are taught to seek the anointing so they can prosper in every way. These vital assets are thereby contorted and distorted in an attempt to fit them into a capitalistic framework that is incapable of containing them.

Several denouncements of the teachings of Word of Faith theology emerge from the biblical hermeneutics (interpretive framework) of its adherents. As evidenced throughout this study, prosperity preachers regularly cite Scriptures out of context to develop and justify their theology. The preachers view the entire Bible, from Genesis to Revelation, as God's redemptive plan for humankind. Since every verse of the Bible is part of God's larger plan, each verse is able to stand on its own as propositional revelation. Therefore, context is not necessary for faithful interpretation. Word of Faith preachers contend that their preaching is biblical because they use texts from the Bible by which to justify it. But not all preaching that uses Scripture is biblical.

Black people, more so than any people in the world, should be aware of the inherent dangers associated with using Scripture out of context. Scriptures were used by slave owners and slave masters to justify the enslavement and oppression of Africans in America. By experience, black people know that when taken out of context, Scriptures can be used to justify the most heinous practices imaginable. Therefore, black people in particular should be suspicious of any preaching that consistently fails to consider context—even when the preaching sounds like good news. If we believe that consideration of biblical context is an essential component of biblical preaching, we cannot classify Word of Faith theology (particularly as it relates to teaching about money and health) as biblical. And if Word of Faith theology is not biblical, then hearers of Word theology who give tithes and offerings, expecting God always to multiply their giving by one hundredfold, are doing so without sound, contextual biblical justification.

Lack of biblical justification can explain the inconsistency of results that followers of Word preaching experience. Many people believe they have been financially and physically blessed (healed of sickness or disease) when they have sown seed into select ministries.[1] At the same time, many other people believe they have not benefited from adherence to Word of Faith teachings.[2]

Inconsistent results can also be explained by the limited impact of positive thinking. Critics of Kenyon believe he developed his teachings by combining the positive thinking teachings of humanism (systems or ways of thinking in which human interest, values, and reason are dominate) with Christian Scriptures. If the teachings of the Word of Faith movement are simply Christianized humanism, then the results of the teachings vary according to abilities, gifts, motivation, socioeconomic status, education, and availability of opportunities of the persons putting them to practice. However, if the teachings are godly promises (and if God were not sovereign), then all people who believe and practice the teachings should be financially wealthy and physically healthy.

By recognizing that many Word of Faith teachings and sermons (namely those that promise financial wealth and perfect physical health) are unbiblical, many of the claims of Word preachers are rendered invalid. Without a sound biblical foundation, Word theology and preaching can be compared to a house of cards that topples upon itself with the slightest touch. If the teachings are unbiblical, then the poor and disenfranchised can once again be seen and valued as children of God rather than being viewed as misguided, uninformed, and unfaithful. If the teachings are unbiblical, Jesus' constant awareness of and care for the poor during his earthly ministry can be used as a model for Christians in the twenty-first century, rather than his supposed wealth. If the teachings are unbiblical, God's sovereignty can once again be embraced and God's obligation to act according to Word teachings, dispelled. If the teachings are unbiblical, believers can be assured they are not always at fault when they experience health problems or encounter financial difficulty. If the teachings are unbiblical, making confessions only for one's own welfare or the welfare of one's own family becomes a model of selfish ambition rather than Christian duty.

If the teachings are unbiblical, Kenyon's classification of sense knowledge as knowledge that comes from books and revelation knowledge as knowledge that comes from God can be refuted. Children of God with gifts of God write books through the grace of God. The Spirit of God can be found within the pages of books other than the Bible. And if the teachings are unbiblical, the importance of prophetic preaching returns to the fore.

Without the absolute promises of God for the attainment of wealth and good health, the responsibility for assuring equitable distribution of the earth's resources, health care, food, adequate and affordable housing, educational opportunity, and safety once again becomes the shared responsibility of all humanity through the power of God, including the body of Christ. Those of us who claim to be followers of Christ must assume our duties as the eyes, ears, hands, feet, and voices of Christ on earth. We must celebrate God's goodness with the unselfish nature of our daily lives in addition to the praise on our lips.

Affirmations and Reconstruction of Faith

The question may arise at this point, if many of the teachings of Word of Faith theology are unbiblical, then what is left? What is a person to do who has believed this theology but who now questions its veracity? Is the unwavering faith that adherents of the prosperity gospel have developed to be left in shambles? Or can believers maintain their faith in God even though they question many of the core tenants of the prosperity gospel?

Such a person has only to return to the wisdom of the word and allow a fresh reading of the Bible to point them toward God once again. The many interactions of God with the people in the Scriptures inform us of the complexity of an omnipotent, omniscient, and omnipresent God. When reading the Old Testament, there can be no question that the God of Israel is a miracle-working God. God brought the people of Israel out of slavery, provided for their every need, and delivered them from Pharaoh's army by enabling Moses to part the sea. God delivered Daniel, blessed Abraham and Sarah, empowered Deborah and Barak, and provided hope for Naomi in a seemingly hopeless situation. The God of the Hebrew Bible is a miracle-working God.

In the New Testament, the gift of salvation through the person and work of Jesus Christ provides us with unconditional love and acceptance, forgiveness, and grace. Jesus met the needs of the people he encountered by healing their physical infirmities and attending to their spiritual needs. At the same time, Christ's life provides a model for living with accountability to God to love our neighbors as we love ourselves. The gift of the Holy Spirit we find in the Bible serves as God's presence in our hearts, neighbors, and world in general to teach us the wisdom and will of God in our daily lives.

One of the most important ways that Word of Faith adherents can reconstruct their faith is by reassessing the relationship between God, the Bible, and pastoral authority. While we as Christians believe the Bible is the word of God, we must always remember it is not God. The words of the Bible can be used to glorify God and represent the will of God for our lives. The words of the Bible can also be used to castigate, subjugate, manipulate, and oppress. While many preachers are called by God to preach to the people of God, they are first and foremost human. Preachers of all denominations and faiths have shortcomings and failures that necessitate that they be held accountable by the communities of faith they serve. Just as they are to seek God for guidance as they teach and preach, the people listening to them must also seek God for discernment of God's truths in the teaching and preaching they receive and convey.

In order to discern whether the words of the Bible represent the word of God or not, Christians must reject the notion that critical thought is the enemy of faith. The mind is a gift of God. While it is possible to reason one's way out of believing in that which one cannot see, it is also possible to reason one's way, through reflection on life experiences (of self and others) and study of the Bible and other literature, into a steadfast and immovable faith. A Christian with steadfast faith is not afraid to ask questions, seek answers, and knock on doors and windows of life's situations and circumstances in search of the ways and wisdom of God. If we believe the mind is a gift of God, we must also believe that God is not disturbed or upset by our questions. Inquiring and critical minds are one of God's many gifts to a fallible, fickle, and sometimes unfaithful humanity. However, God may be disturbed when we check our minds at the doors of our churches and refuse to hold each other accountable for our words and actions.

Reconstructing faith means one has to acknowledge that there *is* a divine economy. We see in the Bible where Jesus multiplied loaves, fish, and wine to meet the needs of the people to whom he was ministering. God *can* bless us miraculously. However, there is no wisdom in creating situations in our lives where God's miraculous intervention is needed on a regular basis, such as assuming a mortgage that our incomes are unable to support. God is sovereign and blesses us according to God's will, not necessarily according to our interpretations of the Word.

Reconstructing faith means acknowledging that Jesus was poor according to the socioeconomic standards of his day. Though he was poor, he was not cursed. Nor are the poor of our day cursed. However, poverty, which denies access to basic needs such as food, clothing, shelter, and educational opportunities, is a curse that can be lifted when all people hold one another and systems accountable. While some poor may bear some responsibility for their economic situations, many of the poor in our world are victims of unjust and unaccountable systems.

Reconstructing faith means acknowledging that God is indeed the source of all blessings, including finances. We must also acknowledge that we do not know or need to know the means God employs to bless us. We simply must have faith that God will meet our needs. However, though God will meet our needs, God is not our own personal genie—existing for the sole purpose of granting all of our wishes.

Reconstructing faith means acknowledging that the anointing of the Holy Spirit is real. The anointing empowers Christians to do the work of God in the world. However, having the anointing of the Holy Spirit does not guarantee wealth and overall prosperity. As in all cases, God determines the degree to which God blesses all people of God. Our role as Christians is to be faithful to our callings whether we become wealthy or not.

Reconstructing faith means believing that there is authority in the name of Jesus. Verbal confessions of faith are a viable means of reinforcing our faith in God. However, we should make our confessions based in God's will versus our own desires to obtain the material trappings of our North American capitalistic context. God is not bound to grant requests that are based on human cultural standards.

Reconstructing faith means believing that God *is* able to heal all sickness and disease. When we pray, we should pray with an unrelenting faith that God is *able* to do all things. However, we should acknowledge that God heals in many different ways. While God can and does heal miraculously, God also uses doctors and therapists to facilitate healing. We must also recognize that just as sickness and disease are not always the result of sin, long-term illness, disability, or even death are not always caused by lack of faith.

Reconstructing faith means believing that Christians are the righteousness of God through Jesus Christ. Because of Jesus, we have been declared righteous in God's sight. Though we can do many of the miraculous works that Jesus did, we are not Jesus' spiritual equals. Though we have been forgiven of our sins, we are not free from sin. We are still imperfect beings who are striving to be more like Jesus every day. God does grant us divine favor. However, divine favor does not negate the importance of personal responsibility.

Reconstructing faith means believing that, in a perfect world, natural heritage would not matter. All people are created and loved equally by God. However, in order to combat the realities of racism and other forms of injustice, we must first acknowledge their existence and our complicity to and participation in them on multiple levels. We must also remind ourselves that the God we serve is a God of justice. As we live our lives, we should do more than seek fulfillment for ourselves. We should love our neighbors by working for their holistic well-being as well as our own.

The Most Consistent Beneficiaries

The people who most consistently profit from Word of Faith theology, especially in larger ministries, are the preachers. Creflo Dollar is but one of hundreds of Word of Faith preachers whose extravagant lifestyles are supported and financed by adherents of Word theology. Dollar owns two Rolls-Royces, two jets, a $3 million mansion, and a $2.5 million apartment in Time Warner Center in New York.[3] While he preaches that money given to God (i.e., to World Changers Church International) should be used to build the kingdom of God, he uses much of the money he earns preaching and teaching the prosperity gospel to enrich himself and his family.

Dollar and other prosperity preachers cite their own financial prosperity as living proof that all hearers can become rich. But this argument is faulty. Most hearers of Word of Faith theology are not charismatic leaders with hundreds or thousands of followers who give money into their ministries—money that, in turn, is used to pay ministerial salaries. Most hearers do not have homes and cars purchased on their behalf. And most hearers do not experience having money literally dropped at their feet on any given day.[4]

Importance of Theological Education

E. W. Kenyon, Kenneth E. Hagin, Kenneth Copeland— none of these Word of Faith preachers completed a formal theological degree program of any sort. None of them were beneficiaries of a seminary education. Though Creflo Dollar earned a bachelor's degree, he also does not have a formal theological education. E. W. Kenyon developed his theology by reading the works and listening to the preaching of his contemporaries. Kenneth Hagin co-opted Kenyon's writings and used Kenyon's theology as the basis of his preaching (see chapter 1, Real Father of the Word of Faith Movement). Kenneth Copeland memorized the preaching of Kenneth Hagin to start his ministry. He later directly incorporated the teachings of Kenyon into his sermons as well.

Many contemporary Word of Faith preachers develop their preaching and teaching using the preaching and teaching of their predecessors, such as Hagin and Kenyon, as a model. Though all preachers approach biblical texts with particular life experiences and beliefs that shape the way we view and interpret texts, the interpretive lenses of Word of Faith preachers prevent them from seeing and understanding the messages contained in the texts themselves. Preachers who are inclined toward Word of Faith theology could benefit greatly from theological education.

To be fair, many preachers engage in responsible, contextual preaching without having had the benefit of a formal theological education. Many preachers in black faith communities, and other faith communities as well, who have not earned theological degrees were fortunate to associate with mentors who innately understood the importance of context in biblical interpretation. These mentors passed along their beliefs and practices to others. Other preachers have searched for and found a wealth of resources on their own, such as biblical commentaries, Bible dictionaries, and encyclopedias that help them better understand the contexts of biblical texts.

Nevertheless, the benefits of formal theological education are numerous. In seminaries and divinity schools, students are not only taught that biblical interpretation must be contextual, but also are exposed to the many options and methods of approaching texts that enable them to extract from the Bible's pages nuggets of hope, comfort, empowerment, critique, and liberation with which to bless the people of God.

A Final Word

Like it or not, Word of Faith theology is interwoven with the theology of many faith cultures in the United States and around the world. Unfortunately, the lack of contextual biblical foundation and its proliferation of an individualistic message makes Word of Faith theology a threat to the black prophetic tradition in particular and to the prophetic religious tradition in general.

In the tradition of the Hebrew Bible prophets, black prophetic preachers have in the past, and continue today, to speak truth to and about power while calling for reform of systems, communities, and individual behavior. The communal nature of black prophetic preaching enabled blacks in the United States to maintain their humanity when the dominant culture sought to deny it. Inspired by black prophetic preachers, people of African descent were able to reject the oppressive preaching and biblical interpretations of the dominant culture in the eighteenth, nineteenth, and twentieth centuries that sought to keep them enslaved and/or relegated them to second-class citizenry. The preaching of ministers such as Henry McNeal Turner and Anne Pauli Murray, combined with grassroots organizing that grew out of the preaching of the civil rights movement, produced social gains for blacks, such as the right to equal education (*Brown vs. Board of Education*) and repeal of Jim Crow laws (equal access to public spaces), and culminated in the US Supreme Court ruling that segregation was unconstitutional in 1956. Other Supreme Court decisions repealed laws in many states that prevented blacks from voting and enjoying basic civil liberties.

The African American prophetic preaching tradition not only helped to liberate African Americans from some systems of oppression, but also inspired and emboldened people all over the world to fight for liberty and justice for all people. The entrance of prosperity theology into African American churches, which already host a diverse array of theological positions, further diminishes the influence of existing prophetic voices and the possibilities of the emergence of new ones.

Responsible and critical members of the body of Christ must not only continue to educate ourselves about Word teachings, but also take up the mantle of "the servant." The servant of Isaiah 53:5 is believed by some biblical scholars to have been a Jeremiah-type prophet who suffered daily as he tried to warn the people of Judah to turn from their evil ways and turn back to God. Assuming the role of "the servant," responsible Christians need to warn the people in our churches of the dangers of the individualistic, capitalistic, justice-averse nature of prosperity gospel. Prosperity gospel threatens to lull good, God-fearing people into self-interested, vainglorious comas in which they live only for their own benefit versus living to serve humanity as well as God. Jesus did instruct his followers to love their neighbors as they love themselves.

Therefore, as faithful and concerned members of the body of Christ, we should:

- Hold our preachers accountable to preach sermons that not only demand personal accountability on all levels, but also demand justice (individual, communal, and systemic) for all people.
- Highlight injustices in the church and the world, and encourage members to use their resources to help others.
- Hold preachers and teachers accountable for interpreting Scripture within its literary, political, and socioeconomic contexts.
- Encourage pastors, preachers, and lay leaders to seek theological education so they can more rightly divide the word.
- Educate other believers about the perils and pitfalls of the prosperity gospel.

- Pray for and work diligently to realize a resurgence of prophetic preaching and prophetic awareness in African American churches in particular, as well as throughout the body of Christ and in the world.

As people of God, God has given us work to do. Let us go into the world and share the good news—Jesus is alive and well in us and in the world. We don't have to be rich or in perfect physical health to please God. Praise be to God!

NOTES

1. Michael Luo, "Preaching the Gospel of Wealth in a Glittery Market, New York," *New York Times*, January 15, 2006. The Anderson family who attend World Changers Church in New York testify in this article about the unexpected blessings they received after they started attending Dollar's services.

2. John Blake, "Dollar and the Gospel," *The Atlanta Journal Constitution*, March 5, 2000, G1.

3. Rick Sherrell, "Cult or Christianity: World Changers Promises Financial Blessing to the Faithful, but Many Leave Disillusioned," December 6, 1997, www.apologeticsindex.org/d11.html (accessed June 5, 2006). Sherrell writes about people who are disillusioned with Dollar's ministry. The people interviewed for the article did not prosper financially while following Dollar's teachings.

4. At Dollar's church in College Park, Georgia, and during his Change conventions, people sometimes make their way to the front of the church or auditorium and lay cash on the steps leading to the pulpit. By engaging in this practice, hearers believe they are sowing seeds into Dollar's ministry with the expectation of receiving a hundredfold return on their gifts.

Bibliography

Bailey, Kenneth E. "The Manger and the Inn: The Cultural Background of Luke 2:7." *The Near East School of Theology Theological Review* 2, no. 2 (1979): 33–44.

Blake, John. "Pastors Choose Sides over Direction of Black Church." *The Atlanta Journal Constitution*, February 15, 2005.

Brown, Colin. "Πτωχος." In *The New International Dictionary of New Testament Theology*, edited by Colin Brown, 825. Exeter, Devon, UK: Paternoster, 1976.

Buess, Bob. *Favor the Road to Success: How to Receive Special Favor with God and People*. New Kensington, PA: Whitaker House, 1975.

Burdick, Donald W. "Hebrews, James, 1, 2 Peter, 1, 2, 3, John, Jude, Revelation." In *The Expositor's Bible Commentary*, edited by James Montgomery Boice, 200. Grand Rapids: Zondervan, 1981.

Calvin, John. *Institutes of the Christian Religion*. Christian Classics Ethereal Library, 2002. http://www.ntslibrary.com/PDF%20Books/Calvin%20Institutes%20of%20Christian%20Religion.pdf (accessed September 20, 2010).

Check into Cash. "What Else Should I Know about Payday Loans?" http://www.checkintocash.com/how-it-works.htm (accessed October 27, 2011).

Coffey, John. "The Abolition of the Slave Trade: Christian Conscience and Political Action." *Cambridge Papers*, no. 2 (2006). http://www.jubilee-centre.org/document.php?id=51 (accessed January 27, 2012).

Copeland, Kenneth. "The Hundredfold Principle." Fort Worth, TX: Kenneth Copeland Ministries, 1983. Audiocassette.

Dollar, Creflo. "The Right Attitude in Recession." College Park, GA: iTunes, 2009.

———. *Understanding the Purpose for the Anointing*. Edmond, OK: Vision Communications, 1992.

Dollar, Creflo Jr. "Christ in You, the Hope of Glory." Pt. 1. College Park, GA: Creflo Dollar Ministries/World Changers Church International, 2006. Compact disc.

———. "Christ in You, the Hope of Glory." Pt. 2. College Park, GA: Creflo Dollar Ministries/World Changers Church International, 2006.

———. "Covenant Understanding of Money." College Park, GA: Creflo Dollar Ministries/World Changers Church International, 2004.

———. "No More Debt." College Park, GA: Creflo Dollar Ministries, 2000.

Emerson, Michael O., and Christian Smith. *Divided by Faith: Evangelical Religion and the Problem of Race in America*. New York: Oxford University Press, 2000.

Fosl, Catherine. *Subversive Southerner: Anne Braden and the Struggle for Racial Justice in the Cold War South*. Lexington: University of Kentucky Press, 2006.

Freedman, David Noel. "Lord of Hosts." In *Eerdmans Dictionary of the Bible*, edited by Tony S. L. Michael, 820–21. Grand Rapids: Eerdmans, 2000.

Green, Joel B., Scot McKnight, and I. Howard Marshall. *Dictionary of Jesus and the Gospels*. Downers Grove, IL: InterVarsity, 1992.

Hagin, Kenneth E. "We Have Been Authorized by Jesus." *Word of Faith*, September 1999, 5–7.

Hanson, Paul. *Isaiah 40–66*. Louisville, KY: John Knox, 1995.

Harrison, Milmon F. *Righteous Riches: The Word of Faith Movement in Contemporary African American Religion*. New York: Oxford University Press, 2005.

Haughton, Jonathan, and Shahidur R. Khandker. *Handbook on Poverty and Inequality*. Washington, DC: The World Bank, 2009.

Henry, Carl Ferdinand Howard. *God, Revelation, and Authority*. 6 vols. Wheaton, IL: Crossway, 1999.

House of Cards. 2009. In CNBC Video, edited by David Faber. http://www.cnbc.com/id/15840232?video=1145392808&play=1 (accessed January 27, 2012).

Hunt, Dave. *Occult Invasion*. Eugene, OR: Harvest House, 1998.

Jerry Savelle Ministries Daily Video. "God Our Source #1." Crowley, TX: iTunes, 2009.

———. "God Our Source #2." iTunes, 2009.

Johnson, Luke Timothy. "The Letter of James," In *The Anchor Bible*, edited by William Foxwell Albright and David Noel Freedman, 302. New York: Doubleday, 1995.

Keith, Chris. "The Role of the Cross in the Composition of the Markan Crucifixion Narrative." *Stone Campbell Journal* 9 (2006): 1, 64–66.

Kenneth Hagin Ministries. "Rhema Ministerial Association International Church Guide." *The Word of Faith*, August 2010, 15–22.

Kenyon, E. W. *Basic Bible Course: The Bible in the Light of Our Redemption.* Lynnwood, WA: Kenyon's Gospel Publishing Society, 1999.

———. *Jesus the Healer.* Lynnwood, WA: Kenyon's Gospel Publishing Society, 1940.

Kenyon, E. W., and Don Gossett. *The Power of Your Words.* New Kensington, PA: Whitaker House, 1977.

Laurentin, Rene. *Les Evangiles De L'enfance Du Christ.* Paris: Descleede Brouwer, 1982.

Lawson, Terry. *How to Study the Word: Taking the Bible from the Pages to the Heart.* Tulsa, OK: Faith Library, 1999.

Leclerc, Thomas L. "Resurrection: Biblical Considerations." *Liturgical Ministry* 18 (2009): 98–99.

Lee, Shayne. *T. D. Jakes: America's New Preacher.* New York: New York University Press, 2005.

Lockman Foundation. 2010. Amplified Bible Background & History. http://www.lockman.org/amplified/ (accessed July 7, 2010).

Long, Thomas G. *Hebrews.* Louisville, KY: Westminster John Knox, 1997.

Luo, Michael. "Preaching the Gospel of Wealth in a Glittery Market, New York." *New York Times,* January 15, 2006.

MacArthur, John. *Charismatic Chaos.* Grand Rapids: Zondervan, 1992.

McGrath, Alister. *A Passion for Truth: The Intellectual Coherence of Evangelicalism.* Downer's Grove, IL: InterVarsity, 1996.

National Association of Social Workers. *Institutional Racism and the Social Work Profession: A Call to Action.* http://www.socialworkers.org/diversity/InstitutionalRacism.pdf, 6 (accessed October 27, 2011).

Perriman, Andrew, and World Evangelical Alliance. Commission on Unity and Truth among Evangelicals. *Faith, Health and Prosperity: A Report on Word of Faith and Positive Confession Theologies by ACUTE* (Evangelical Alliance Commission on Unity and Truth among Evangelicals). Carlisle: Paternoster, 2003.

Poverty and Inequality Analysis. 2010. The World Bank, http://web.worldbank.org/WBSITE/EXTERNAL/TOPICS/EXTPOVERTY/0,contentMDK:22569747~pagePK:148956~piPK:216618~theSitePK:336992,00.html (accessed September 15, 2010).

Preston, Classy. "Spiritual Empowerment: A Closer Look." In *Those Preaching Women: African American Preachers Tackle Tough Questions,* edited by Ella Pearson Mitchell. Valley Forge, PA: Judson, 1996.

Riss, Richard. "The Latter Rain Movement of 1948." *Journal of the Society for Pentecostal Studies* 4, no. 1 (1982).

Roberts, Oral. *The Miracle of Seed-Faith.* Tulsa, OK: Oral Roberts Ministries, 1970.

Rosin, Hanna. "Did Christianity Cause the Mortgage Crisis?" *Atlantic Magazine* (2009). http://www.theatlantic.com/magazine/archive/2009/12/did-christianity-cause-the-crash/7764/2/ (accessed January 27, 2012).

Schreiber, Mordecai. "The Real 'Suffering Servant': Decoding a Controversial Passage in the Bible." *Jewish Bible Quarterly* 37, no. 1 (January–March 2009): 35–44.

Sherrell, Rick. "Cult or Christianity: World Changers Promises Financial Blessing to the Faithful, but Many Leave Disillusioned." December 6, 1997. Apologetics Index, http://www.apologeticsindex.org/d11.html (accessed December 13, 2011).

Sherrod, Shirley. 2010. Shirley Sherrod: The Full Video. NAACP 20th Annual Freedom Fund Banquet, YouTube, http://www.youtube.com/watch?v=E9NcCa_KjXk (accessed October 4, 2010).

Simmons, Dale H. *E. W. Kenyon and the Postbellum Pursuit of Peace, Power and Plenty*. Studies in Evangelicalism. No. 13. Lanham, MD: Scarecrow, 1997.

Smedley, Audrey, and Brian D. Smedley. "Race as Biology Is Fiction, Racism as a Social Problem Is Real." *American Psychologist* 60 (2005).

The State of Black America 2010. "Jobs: Responding to the Crisis." 2010. National Urban League, http://www.thechicagourbanleague.org/732310130204959623/lib/732310130204959623/EXECUTIVE%20SUMMARY%20StateBlkAmerica.pdf (accessed September 20, 2010).

Stonecipher, Elliott. "Study: The New Orleans Population in Peril." CBS News, Jan. 27, 2006. www.cbsnews.com/stories/2006/01/27/katrina/main1247418.shtml (accessed February 18, 2006).

Synan, Vincent. "Memphis 1994: Miracle and Mandate." *Reconciliation*, no. 1 (1998).

The Tithing Hoax. "The Prosperity Gospel—When Paying Tithes Goes Wrong." http://thetithinghoax.com/the-prosperity-gospel-when-paying-tithes-goes-wrong/ (accessed October 1, 2011).

Van Leeuwen, Raymond. *The Book of Proverbs*. The New Interpreter's Bible. Vol. 5. Nashville: Abingdon, 1997.

Way, Kenneth C. "Donkey Domain: Zechariah 9:9 and Lexical Semantics." *Journal of Biblical Literature* 129, no 1 (Spring 2010): 114.

Whitacre, Rodney A. *John*. Downers Grove, IL: InterVarsity, 1999.

Winston, Bill. "Faith in the Name of Jesus." Bill Winston Ministries, 2009.

———. "No More Toil." Bill Winston Ministries, 2007. http://www.podcast.tv/video-episodes/no-more-toil-14049200.html (accessed January 27, 2012).

———. 2008. "Understanding Our Divinity." In *Kingdom Mentality*, Bill Winston Ministries. http://bwmbroadcast.org/player/flash?stream=BW591_2.mp4 (accessed September 17, 2010).

Witherington, B. "The Birth of Jesus." In *The Dictionary of Jesus and the Gospels*, edited by Joel B. Green, Scot McKnight, and I. Howard Marshall, 993. Downer's Grove, IL: InterVarsity, 1992.